Managerial Decision Cases

Thomas
Finnegan

Director of Academics
– MBA Program

University of Illinois
at Urbana – Champaign

South-Western College Publishing
Thomson Learning™

Australia • Canada • Mexico • Singapore • Spain • United Kingdom • United States

Managerial Decision Cases by Thomas R. Finnegan

Team Director: Dave Shaut
Acquisitions Editor: Rochelle J. Kronzek
Production Editor: Mark Sears
Marketing Manager: Larry Qualls
Cover Design: Jennifer Lambert
Cover Image: © 2000 PhotoDisc, Inc.
Manufacturing Coordinator: Doug Wilke
Printer: Phoenix Color

Printed in the United States of America
1 2 3 4 5 03 02 01 00

For more information contact South-Western College Publishing, 5101 Madison Road, Cincinnati, Ohio, 45227 or find us on the Internet at http://www.swcollege.com

For permission to use material from this text or product, contact us by
• **telephone: 1-800-730-2214**
• **fax: 1-800-730-2215**
• **web: http://www.thomsonrights.com**

ISBN: 0-324-02011-2 package text with disk
ISBN: 0-324-02338-3 text only

This book is printed on acid-free paper.

Managerial Decision Cases

Table of Contents

**Managerial Decision
Cases**

Preface

Decision Making and Strategic Planning Focus

According to a recent Institute of Management Accounting (IMA)–supported research report, "In the past 10 years, the characterization of management accountants in leading edge companies has grown from 'bean counter' and 'corporate cop,' on the periphery of business decision making, to 'business partner' and valued team member, at the very center of strategic activity."[1] The study also reports that 80 percent of management accountants who responded to the survey spend more time analyzing information, making decisions, and planning strategically than they did five years ago (p. 5).

In response to these changes, the cases in this book do not focus on debits and credits. Rather, students are placed in situations requiring strategic thinking and decision-making skills. The cases are structured so that students spend more time thinking critically and less time sifting through institutional detail.

The change in focus does not mean that students will not be required to apply what is considered to be the common body of knowledge in management accounting. The casebook topics are the same as those found in most traditional managerial accounting textbooks, and are presented in the same order. A partial list of topics includes basic cost concepts, costing systems, activity-based costing and management, break-even analysis, budgeting, standard costing, variance analysis, responsibility accounting, performance evaluation, relevant costs, variable costing, capital budgeting, and inventory.

---

[1] *Counting More, Counting Less: Transformations in the Management Accounting Profession* (IMA, 1999): p. 1

Pedagogically, this book can be used as a supplement to accounting and business texts, a stand-alone casebook, or a vehicle that facilitates in-class active learning exercises.

Account, Analyze, and Act—The Three As

In many cases, students must *account* for revenues and costs, *analyze* the accounted-for information, and *act* (that is, make a decision). The cases in this book often involve problems or conflicts such as declining profitability or goal incongruence that require students to think critically and to use knowledge and skills derived from the course. In addition, students make recommendations regarding a firm's course of action. In this respect, students are expanding upon a skill set associated with the traditional accounting function (scorekeeping) to include decision-making expertise. Although the cases are fictional, the settings represent real-world scenarios.

Spreadsheets and Database

Over half of the cases can be solved, in part, using computer spreadsheet software programs such as Excel and Lotus. The numbers in the cases can be manipulated to facilitate students' learning by creating a variety of "as-if" scenarios. The spreadsheets can also be used to create forward-looking statements so that students can think strategically and become proactive decision makers. When appropriate, the solutions manual provides answers to the case questions in spreadsheet form.

A chapter in the casebook includes cases involving an Access database. Students can download data from the database, or the instructor can distribute the data in a form of his or her choice. The Access database gives students experience working with a database software program as well as an abundance of information that can be analyzed and interpreted.

Custom Publishing

South-Western College Publishing's customized publishing program allows one to publish a casebook in a variety of forms that will enhance the adopter's text, coursework, and in-class activities. For more information on how to create your customized casebook, please contact your South-Western College sales representative.

Acknowledgements

I am grateful to those who helped produce this casebook. Specifically, I would like to thank Rochelle Kronzek, Leslie Kauffman, Mark Sears, Jacqueline Blakley, and Jennifer Elworth for their editorial and technical assistance; Prakaijit Sura-amornkul for constructing the Access database; and Gridtiga Sirivallop and Jackie Wong for their assistance in generating solutions to the cases. In addition, I would like to recognize the feedback provided by accountancy and MBA students at the University of Illinois, Urbana-Champaign.

About the Author

Thomas R. Finnegan
J.D., Ph.D., C.P.A.

Thomas R. Finnegan is the director of academics for the master of business administration (MBA) program at the University of Illinois, Urbana-Champaign. As a member of the accountancy faculty at Illinois, he is currently teaching undergraduate and graduate managerial and financial accounting courses. He has received numerous teaching awards, including the university's Executive MBA Outstanding Teaching Award.

Finnegan holds a Ph.D. in accountancy from the University of Illinois, a juris doctor degree from the University of Illinois, and a bachelor of science degree in mechanical engineering from Purdue University. He is an attorney-at-law and a certified public accountant.

He has worked for the Big Five accounting firm, Arthur Andersen, the law firm, Winston & Strawn (Chicago), and the former Fortune 500 company, CBI Industries.

For All — You Know Who You Are

Chapter 1

Introduction

Case 1.1

The Perfect Game

"What is the most important part of any basketball game?" This was another in a long line of riddles that Jim posed to Fred every time their teams competed in conference play. As Fred watched the teams go through warm-up drills, he began to think about Jim's question.

The intellectual interplay was typical of the way things started when the "significant seven" met to renew their friendly rivalry. Of the seven, three (Fred, Michelle, and Ralph) had graduated from the host college, while the other four (Jim, Mary, Mike, and Bill) had graduated from the visiting school.

After college, all but one took jobs and purchased homes in the town of the college they had attended. Some of their friends believed that the seven thought that commencement meant the commencement of a lifelong athletic rivalry between the two schools. Fortunately, over the years, the rivalry evolved into a congenial sport of spectating.

Fred continued to ponder Jim's riddle until his restless friends began teasing him. He finally ventured an answer: "Coaching is the most important part of any game." Jim declared, "No." Fred quickly retorted, "Players." There was no reaction from Jim. Fred tried again, "Referees!" Jim said, "Try again." The third rejection triggered a different reaction. Fred stood up, started toward the exit, and said, "I'll be back." This drew the others' attention, and, after some time, they began to wonder whether they would see Fred for the duration of the game.

After about 20 minutes, Fred returned with a plastic bag in his right hand and a smile on his face. He said to Jim, "I've got the answer in this bag." Everyone in the group looked, eager to see what he had. Fred paused, reached in the bag, and quickly pulled out a small hand-sized version of a college basketball. He proudly asserted, "A basketball is the most important part of any basketball game. Without the ball, the game couldn't be played." Jim answered, "Absolutely! Without the ball, we would never have a chance to see what we hope to see every year — the perfect game."

This year, Jim's annual riddle contest spurred the following series of questions and statements.

Mary: "If the basketball is so important, why isn't the ball prohibitively expensive? How many basketballs does a team use in a season? And what is the price of each ball? Aren't most balls made out of leather? Leather isn't that expensive. How much does it cost to produce a ball?"

Bill: "Most basketballs are made from leather or rubber. However, I would think that with the advent of technology a new material could improve upon the current basketball's performance at a cost savings. Don't you think that schools would be interested in a cheaper basketball? If I were to develop a new material for the ball, how long would it take to produce the new ball? How much would it cost and how long would it take to change the manufacturing process so that the new ball could be produced in large quantities?"

Ralph: "I don't think the ball is the most important part of this game. Fans are number one! Without paying spectators, there would be no money to pay the coaches, referees, and ushers. Nor would there be any money to heat, light, build, and repair the facilities. How many people are attending today's game? How does the school plan for a game such as this?"

Michelle: "I went to the Chicago Bulls game last week. I can't believe how much money the professional basketball players are paid! How many tickets must be sold before the owners break even? Will the school make money from today's ticket sales?"

Mike: "I think the school will make a profit, and I'll tell you why. I read in the newspaper yesterday that the athletic department is going to build a new arena. How will the school pay for it? Are we paying for the new building? What percentage of the ticket price will go to capital construction and improvements?"

Discussion Questions

1. What type of management accounting information would be needed to answer the questions posed by Mary, Bill, Ralph, Michelle, and Mike?

2. What type of management accounting activities are associated with the questions posed by Mary, Bill, Ralph, Michelle, and Mike?

3. What types of organizations need management accounting information? A firm that produces basketballs? A college or university?

Managerial, Financial , and Tax Accounting

Case 1.2

Reconcilable Differences

"My word!" exclaimed Erin. "I didn't think we were going to have to track the accounts of two companies under three different accounting systems. I can't believe managerial, financial, and tax accounting income differ by that much."

Erin Reasonik worked in the consulting department of a well-known accounting firm. Her group specialized in developing and maintaining information systems for large multinational companies that have merged within the last five years. These firms discovered that many of their accounting functions could be outsourced at a substantial savings. In Erin's situation, even though the newly merged entertainment and cable companies would be headquartered in New York, the primary accounting data and work would exist in Tulsa, Oklahoma. Tulsa was an up-and-coming city that seemed to attract many bright and talented young accountants who enjoyed the lifestyle the city provided.

"All right," she said, "let's get to work." She asked her co-worker Brad Busby to provide her with the most recent list of income statement accounts, and Brad handed her the following report.

	2000-2001 ($ billions)	
	Entertainment Company	**Cable Company**
Sales	$20	$25
Direct materials	4	1
Direct labor	3	2
Overhead (OH)		
Financial accounting	0	0
Tax accounting	8	13
Managerial accounting	5	8
Selling	2	5
Administration	3	4

He told Erin that the final report, which would contain amounts for financial accounting overhead, was expected to be completed within two weeks. He explained that the delay was due to the merged firm waiting for opinions from another CPA firm regarding: 1) whether the merger-related expenses should be capitalized or expensed, and 2) appropriate cost allocation methods to be applied by the new company.

Erin said she was confused by the zero amount for financial accounting overhead and that rather than waiting two weeks, they should prepare pro-forma financial statements based on the information they did have. Erin then asked Brad for another set of data that included merger-related overhead accounts. He provided her with the following.

Merger-Related Expenses ($ billions)

Training costs	0.50
Advertising costs	1.00
Incidental repairs	0.25
Severance payments	12.50

Non-Merger-Related Overhead: Financial Reporting ($ billions)

Entertainment Company	Cable Company
4	7

Erin turned to Brad and said, "You going anywhere for lunch?" Brad said, "Of course, I always go to Bin-Bins for turtle soup on Wednesday." She responded, "Do they deliver?" Brad said, "I'll check." Erin then replied, "Make that two turtle soups. We are staying here and finishing this one before the end of the week."

Discussion Questions

1. Prepare income statements for each company using the managerial, financial, and tax accounts. List your assumptions.

2. Provide a schedule that reconciles the accounts.

3. What other sources or types of information should be included in the information system? Specifically, what other information would improve the decision-making ability of the newly merged firm?

Case 1.3

Nature's Best Bagel

Nature's Best Bagel, Inc., (NB Bagel), is the largest producer of bagels in Denver, Colorado. The firm's biggest seller, the All Natural, is sold to more than 100 coffee shops and grocery stores in the Denver area. The firm markets its bagels as being the healthiest among competing bagels. The owners felt this strategy would reach the area's largest demographic group, baby boomers. In addition to being health conscious, NB Bagel is a good corporate citizen and a major contributor of food to local Habitat for Humanity construction sites.

NB Bagel, which began operating in 1990, experienced 20 percent growth in sales and income during the first five years of its operation. However, return on assets (ROA), return on sales (ROS), and profits have recently declined. This downward trend has come to the attention of the firm's CEO, Janet Gustafson. Janet has taken it upon herself to conduct a personal inquiry so that she can understand why profits are falling even though sales continue to be strong.

Janet's first stop was the accounting department. She discovered that, though the accounting system was computerized, no one was able to explain how costs were assigned to bagels as they flowed through the manufacturing process. Janet left the department disappointed and confused but still determined to find answers to NB Bagel's problems. The next day, she called her chief operating officer, Bob Thomas, and asked if he could help her understand the firm's business processes and cost structure.

Bob came to NB Bagel after five years with a consulting firm that specialized in process value analysis (PVA). He recommended they begin by observing and diagramming the manufacturing process. Bob told Janet that he would then classify activities as being value-added (VA) and nonvalue-added (NVA), identify cost drivers for the nonvalue-added activities, and list ways the firm could reduce or eliminate nonvalue-added costs.

During the next week, Janet and Bob observed the manufacturing operation, starting with delivery of raw material, and ending with shipment of bagels. The following is what the two observed.

Raw Materials

The basic ingredients for the All Natural bagel are sugar, flour, yeast, salt, eggs, and cornmeal. All ingredients, with the exception of cornmeal, are received from an Estes Park, Colorado, supplier. NB Bagel pays shipping costs and insurance for the one-hour trip from the Estes Park warehouse. The key ingredient, cornmeal, is what makes the All Natural so popular. NB Bagel receives cornmeal from its Des Moines, Iowa, manufacturing facility, which it purchased from a family after discovering the family's unique patented cornmeal production process. The trip from Des Moines to Denver takes about eight hours.

Testing and Storage

Quality-control testing begins when ingredients arrive at the Denver facility. It takes about 15 minutes to inspect everything except the cornmeal, which takes about two hours to test and inspect. The rigorous testing procedures are undertaken so that the quality of the key ingredient is not compromised. After testing, the ingredients are sent to storage and remain there for an average of five days.

Production

The production process consists of ten steps:

1. Water and yeast are combined, mixed, and allowed to set for ten minutes.
2. Sugar, salt, and flour are added to the mix and blended for another 10 minutes.
3. Flour is added until the dough is firm, at which time it is kneaded until smooth.
4. The dough is sent to a room that is kept at 85 degrees Fahrenheit. It takes 10 minutes to transfer the dough to and from the warm room. The dough rises for one hour.

5. The dough is sent through the adjacent cutting, rolling, and forming machine, which produces individual bagels.

6. The bagels are sent back to the warm room, where they wait anywhere from 10 to 30 minutes.

7. The bagels are transported via a four-wheeled motorized cart and boiled in a cooking facility five minutes away.

8. After boiling, the bagels are placed on a large conveyor in the cooking facility, dipped in cornmeal, and brushed with egg yolk.

9. The bagels are baked at 400 degrees Fahrenheit for 30 minutes.

10. After the bagels are baked, they are placed on a cooling rack located between the ovens and shipping.

Shipping

After the bagels have cooled, they are placed in recycled-paper cartons containing either 12, 24, or 48 bagels. The recycled cartons are more expensive than regular cartons. Although consumers never see the cartons, conservation is part of the firm's mission. To ensure quality, the bagels are inspected as they are placed in the cartons. Inspectors seal the boxes with a wax stamp that is dated and labeled "NB Bagel." Filled cartons are then placed in the delivery trucks, which travel an average of two hours. Loading time is 30 to 90 minutes.

Discussion Questions

1. Diagram NB Bagel's manufacturing process. The process should start with delivery of raw materials and end with final shipment of goods.

2. On a separate sheet of paper, list activities in the manufacturing process (such as moving and storage).

3. Classify the activities in question 2 as being value-added (VA) or nonvalue-added (NVA).

4. List ways NB Bagel could reduce or eliminate nonvalue-added activities.

Case 1.4

Loft Apartments

Loft Apartments, Inc., leases 900 one- to three-bedroom apartments in the suburbs of Atlanta, Georgia. It has as few as 50 and as many as 200 units in eight locations. The apartments are popular because each unit contains a loft that can be used as a study area, office, or bedroom.

In the last five years, business has been very good. However, Doug Baxter, the firm's controller and chief operating officer, can't explain why certain apartment complexes are having difficulties meeting payroll even though occupancy is high. This is especially true for the Marietta complex.

Doug graduated from a local university with an accounting degree. He was interested in real estate management and began his career with Loft Apartments, Inc., as a rental consultant. After two years, he became Marietta's accountant and operations director reporting to the general manager of the complex. He submitted monthly financial reports to this manager, who audited and forwarded the statements to the firm's controller. The controller consolidated the statements and provided copies to the firm's only shareholders, Kent and Cheryl Bianca. After Doug had been with the firm for 10 years, the Biancas promoted him to controller and chief operating officer.

In 1998, Amy Coldwell, the firm's vice president in charge of development and strategic planning, approached Loft's owners with an idea. She thought the firm's unique loft design and its construction system, which was owned by Kent and Cheryl, was sure to

11

succeed in other cities. Amy proposed a public offering of 100,000 shares of stock. The proceeds would be used to build apartments in the suburbs of Baltimore and New Orleans.

Kent asked for an opinion from longtime friend John Meckler, who worked with the investment banking firm of Johnson and Meriman. At their weekly lunch meeting, John said he and his firm would participate in the offering by providing capital and services only if Kent could assure him that Loft Apartments, Inc., was in solid financial condition. Kent told John that he would provide him with financial statements the next time they met.

The next day, Kent called Doug and asked him for financial statements for each of the last 24 months, as well as one- and two-year summaries. Kent said he was serious about pursuing Amy's expansion idea and needed financial statements that would support the stock offering. Kent also promised that Doug would receive 5 percent of the stock offering.

Doug worked on the request all day and into the night. On Tuesday night at 9:00, he left his office with the intention of driving straight home. However, he was still plagued by questions about Marietta's cash-flow situation. So, on the way home, he took a slight detour and drove past the Marietta complex. To his surprise, only about one-half to two-thirds of the apartments appeared to be occupied. This was contrary to what he expected, given the high occupancy-rate reports he received from Marietta's general manager, Paul Wentworth.

Doug had a restless night of sleep. When he arrived at work the next day, he called Lois Gennings, Marietta's accountant, and asked her to lunch. Like Doug, Lois had a degree in accounting and had passed the Certified Management Accountant (CMA) exam.

Doug showed Lois the consolidated statement he had prepared (see the end of this case study) and asked her whether she would attest to the Marietta portion of the statement. She was silent. He asked her whether the complex still had cash-flow problems. She responded, "Yes." He said, "How can that be? Your occupancy is very high."   Lois looked at the floor while telling Doug that the figures for Marietta were inflated. She said she submitted the correct report, but Paul Wentworth altered the figures so that the complex would show 90-percent occupancy. Paul received a $10,000 bonus if this figure was attained. Lois said she didn't do anything for fear of losing her job.

Doug leaned back in his chair and said, "If you don't say anything, you will keep your job, I will recommend that you become operations director, and I will receive my 5-percent share." Lois told him she would keep quiet and left the lunch in a quandary.

Discussion Questions

1. What should Lois do?

2. What do the Institute of Management Accountants' *Objectives of Management Accounting* require her to do?

Loft Apartments, Inc.

Atlanta, Georgia

Monthly Income Statement

3/31/20XX

	Total Units	**3/31/20XX**
Rental revenue:		
Decatur	50	$ 37,500
East Point	75	52,500
Marietta	200	130,000
Peachtree City	175	122,500
Riverdale	75	67,500
Roswell	150	97,500
Smyrna	50	50,000
Stone Mountain	125	75,000
Possible rental revenue		$632,500
Less: Vacancies		80,000
Actual rental revenue		$552,500
Operating expenses:		
Salaries and wages		$113,850
Real estate taxes		63,250
Insurance		56,925
Utilities		44,275
Repairs and maintenance		12,650
Total expenses		$290,950
Operating income		$261,550
Less: Debt service		145,980
Net income		$115,570

Chapter 2

Basic Concepts

Product Costs

Case 2.1

Café B-Day!: Part I

Café B-Day! is a restaurant in the suburbs of a large Southwestern city. It specializes in creating birthday party experiences for people of all ages. All revenue is derived from parties for which the restaurant provides classic party food, such as beverages, cake, and pizza, and fun in the form of a video-game parlor and an indoor swimming pool.

The founders and owners of the restaurant, Terri and Joshua Bochetti, were delighted by the restaurant's early successes, but have become concerned about recent declining profits. Terri believes the problem relates to their sales and marketing strategy. Joshua disagrees; he believes the problem comes from production inefficiencies. So, in order to find ways to improve the restaurant's profits and to reconcile their opposing views, the couple called Terri's sister, Susan Chadwick, who is an accountant with a local CPA firm. They asked if she would conduct a strategic operational audit of the firm. Susan agreed and scheduled a meeting with her sister and brother-in-law for the following week. She asked that in the visit, the couple convey to her their strategy, describe the restaurant's operations, and provide her with a price list and set of financial statements.

When they met, Terri told Susan that their strategy was to provide high-quality birthday experiences at reasonable cost. The couple then took Susan on a tour of the restaurant floor, kitchen, and back office. She observed three distinct sections of the restaurant: the eating area, game room, and pool. The eating area was the largest part of the restaurant, covering more than 2,500 square feet. While in the kitchen, Susan learned that both the cake and the pizza were made from scratch. She remarked, "You make birthday cakes and pizza from scratch?" Terri responded, "Yes. We feel that is an important part of our quality program."

After the kitchen tour, Joshua gave Susan a price list, and the three of them sat at one of the restaurant tables. The list consisted of three items: B-Day! Plans 1, 2, and 3. Plan 1, the lowest-priced option, consisted of beverage, cake, and game room privileges. Under the second plan, pizza was provided in addition to the items in Plan 1. Plan 3, the most expensive option, consisted of beverage, pizza, cake, game room privileges, and pool access.

Terri then handed Susan a set of financial statements and a cost statement that showed how costs and prices for the three plans were derived. The cost statement is shown here.

Schedule I:

Café B-Day!

Basic Data

Cost and Price per Customer

Food	Plan 1	Plan 2	Plan 3
Beverages[1]	$ 0.50	$ 0.50	$ 0.50
Cake[2]	2.50	2.50	2.50
Pizza[3]	—	4.00	4.00
Activity			
Game room[4]	3.00	3.00	3.00
Swimming pool[5]	—	—	6.00
Total cost	$6.00	$10.00	$16.00
Markup of 25% (gratuity not included)	1.50	2.50	4.00
Price	$7.50	$12.50	$20.00

Schedule II: Formulas
Amounts were derived from monthly averages using the following formulas:
[1] Beverage cost (free refills) = (number of glasses × cost per glass) / number of customers
[2] Cake cost (per slice) = (number of cakes × direct material cost per cake) / number of slices
[3] Pizza cost (two slices) = (2 × direct material cost per pizza) / number of slices
[4] Game cost = ([1/2 × labor cost] + [utility cost × 1/4]) / number of customers
[5] Pool cost = ([1/2 × labor cost] + [utility cost × 3/4]) / number of pool customers

Utility costs were allocated based on the relative amount of occupied square footage.

Susan thanked her sister and brother-in-law for the tour and information. As she left the restaurant, she asked the couple whether they had noticed anything unusual over the past several months. Joshua immediately said, "Yes. We got off to a great start. Everyone chose Plan 3. However, while the number of parties and customers remains relatively stable, most customers are now choosing Plan 1 or Plan 2. In fact, most prefer just cake and games."

Discussion Questions

1. Assume Susan approaches you and asks you what you think about Café B-Day!'s product costing methods. How would you respond?

2. Now assume Susan asks you about the couple's strategic plan. What would you say?

3. Make five recommendations that would improve the restaurant's profits.

Products, Services, and Experiences

Case 2.2

Café B-Day!: Part II

Café B-Day! drew Susan Chadwick's interest immediately. She wanted to understand why profits for the restaurant were falling. Was owner Joshua Bochetti right? Did the problem relate to production inefficiencies? Was her sister Terri's belief—that the problem was with the restaurant's strategy of providing high-quality experiences at a reasonable cost—well-founded? Could both Joshua and Terri be correct?

Susan began looking at the shifting product mix. Customers were moving away from the highest-priced party plan of beverages, pizza, cake, games, and swimming to the basic plan of beverages, cake, and games. She realized that customer preferences would not change after she learned that Joshua and Terri had tried to increase demand for the most expensive package through an extensive ad campaign that turned out to be ineffective.

Susan decided to focus on Café B-Day!'s cost of producing goods, services, and experiences. She thought that if she understood the restaurant's cost structure better, she might be able to justify a price change. In fact, she explored the idea of charging a flat fee for the Café experience. Although more and more customers chose not to swim, they were still able to take advantage of the restaurant's ambiance, which was enhanced by the pool and its surrounding area. The party experience was also enhanced by entertaining servers, a disc jockey, employees dressed as life-sized cartoon characters, and free virtual-game glasses. Susan thought each customer should be charged for the memorable activities and sensations.

After several iterations, she came up with the following pricing scheme.

	Experience Fee	Other Charges
Plan 1 (beverages, cake, and games)	$5.00	$7.50
Plan 2 (Plan 1 plus pizza)	$5.00	$12.50
Plan 3 (Plan 2 plus swimming)	$5.00	$20.00

She arrived at the $5.00 experience fee as follows:

Labor (servers, cartoon characters)	$2.00
Music (disc jockey)	0.50
Building and equipment depreciation	1.00
Utilities	0.50
Miscellaneous overhead	1.00
Total fee	$5.00

Susan has asked for your assistance.

Discussion Questions

1. What are the strengths and weaknesses of Susan's approach? Discuss the efficacy of charging for experiences.

2. Discuss how an experience-based economy would affect cost and managerial accounting systems.

Chapter 3

Activity Cost Behavior

Cost Behavior: Flexible, Committed, and Discretionary Costs

Case 3.1

Movies, Etc.

Meet, eat, take a seat, and repeat! This was Stephen Plot's slogan for the Movies, Etc., expansion plan. Stephen was about to approach his friend Sara Reid, a loan officer at First Merchant National Bank, in an effort to raise $500,000 in capital needed to update his theater.

Stephen was the owner of Movies, Etc., a 15-screen movie theater in the Finger Lakes region of upstate New York. Recently, he had developed an expansion plan that, in his words, "will put all the small- and medium-sized movie theaters out of business." He also believed that his new concept would take customers away from local restaurants and drinking establishments.

Stephen didn't mind rubbing people the wrong way. In fact, he told several of his employees that he gauged his success by the number of personal attacks he received from local merchants. He felt that the more merchants disliked him, the better he must be doing.

His relationship with the general public was a different story. Stephen was very popular with the public at large. He donated tickets to local children's clubs and charities for disadvantaged youth; created teen discount nights in which teenagers were allowed into the theater for half price; gave away popcorn on Tuesday nights; and sponsored local youth and adult soccer, softball, and volleyball teams.

Stephen was naturally aggressive and always thought big, so his new expansion plan did not come as a surprise to anyone. His plan, which is outlined here, consisted of the following four phases: Phase 1: *Meet;* Phase 2: *Eat;* Phase 3: *Take a Seat;* and Phase 4: *Repeat.*

Phase 1: *Meet*

The current lobby would be expanded to include a 30- by 40-foot social area with an adjacent juice bar and snack shop. The juice bar would include such items as soft drinks, mineral water, and fruit juices. Stephen and his managers were strongly opposed to serving beverages containing any alcohol. And besides, he didn't think he could obtain a liquor license, since several members of the local liquor board were restaurant and bar owners who had historically opposed any of his plans. He was also exploring the possibility of handing over the juice bar to a local health food store, Raspberry Hills Co-op.

The expansion plan blueprints revealed a large enclosed snack shop. Hard and soft candies, chocolate snacks, and health-food snacks from Raspberry Hills would be a part of the daily fare. The juice bar and snack shop would be situated near the entrance on the edges of the social area, which included a parquet floor, televisions, and music.

Phase 2: *Eat*

The current Movies, Etc., facility would also be expanded to include a restaurant serving pizza, hamburgers, and hot dogs. The restaurant's name, "No Commercials," refers to Stephen's plan for fast-serve meals that contain no unwanted interruptions in the dining experience. Inside the restaurant, a public address system would announce which movies were about to begin and end as well as information about current and future features.

Phase 3: *Take a Seat*

Stephen's plan included five new theaters with stadium seating and food benches. With 20 theaters, Stephen thought he would be able to show foreign, children's, art, and popular movies simultaneously. He wanted to be able to show all first-run movies that were being shown within a 25-mile radius. Two years after the expansion plan was completed, Stephen felt his theater would be so popular that no small (one screen) or medium (two to six screens) theaters would be able to compete with him in the first-run movie market. Instead, he thought these theaters would either go out of business or show second-run films at a substantial discount.

Phase 4: *Repeat*

Under the new plan, if a patron purchased a ticket and at least one food item, he or she would be given an unlimited viewing pass good for that day. The pass was dated and would be distributed by the food and beverage employees. Stephen thought this aspect of his plan would bolster profits because patrons would stay longer and buy more food, which is the highest profit margin item. Currently, 75 percent of Movies, Etc., profits is derived from food sales. Following is a current abbreviated monthly cost statement for Movies, Etc.

Movies, Etc.
Monthly Cost Statement (Abbreviated)
6/30/XX

Item	6/30/XX
Employee salaries and fringe benefits	$25,000
Maintenance	750
Insurance	1,000
Utilities	2,000
Advertising and promotion	3,000
Administrative expenses	1,500
Food and beverage costs	9,000
Depreciation, building, and equipment	500
Movie rental fee	22,250
Total	$65,000

Discussion Questions

1. List all pre-expansion costs for Movies, Etc., and next to each cost, classify the cost as fixed, variable, mixed, step-variable, and step-fixed.

2. Identify all resources that would be required by Stephen Plot's expansion plan. [Suggestion: You should categorize expenditures broadly (for example, restaurant, social area), and beneath each category provide a list of specific items such as televisions, chairs, and display cases.]

3. What implications does the nature of the resources have for management control and decision making?

4. What do you think of Stephen's plan?

Cost Estimation Using High-Low, Scatterplot, and Regression Methods

Case 3.2

CookieWorld, Inc.

Debra McCarty rushed into Sally Marshall's office and exclaimed, "Oh, no! You are not going to believe this!" Debra had just looked at the regression output shown below and expressed extreme concern about what she had observed.

Regression Output

Minutes per batch[1] = constant + X coefficient × (number of cookies per batch)

Constant	26.476
Standard error of Y estimate	5.560
R squared	0.0572
Number of observations	35
Degrees of freedom	1
X coefficient	-0.448
Standard error of coefficient	0.317
Lower 95%	-1.092
Upper 95%	0.196

[1] Minutes per batch is the length of time required to produce a batch of cookies from scratch.

Sally said to Debra, "Now calm down, Debra. It can't be that bad." Debra responded, "You know that promotion you promised me? Well, you might want to reconsider."

Sally is the owner of CookieWorld, Inc., which is known for high-quality cookies. A significant portion of its profit is derived from the sale of Christmas cookies. Sally was considering changing the firm's strategy in order to reverse the declining profit trend.

She had recently promised Debra a promotion to firm controller and told her that her first assignment was to devise an improved cost accounting system that could pinpoint the "actual cost" of each cookie. Debra thought this would be no problem since she considered herself something of a regression guru. In college, Debra took a statistics class from nationally known professor Dan Roberts, who always received outstanding teaching awards. So, she believed she had this one under control.

Both Debra and Sally thought it was important to know the cost of each cookie for two reasons. First, the firm was experiencing increasing competition in the St. Louis area, where all of the firm's 10 stores were located. All stores but one, which was in Kirkwood, were experiencing shrinking profits. They needed to understand the cost of each type of cookie in order to reformulate the firm's product mix and pricing strategies. Second, Debra and Sally thought that if they could identify which activities or processes caused costs, then the manufacturing process could be reengineered in order to achieve cost reductions.

After several anxious seconds, Sally asked Debra to explain the problem. Debra walked over to Sally's desk, plopped down a computer printout, and pointed to the R-squared statistic. She said, "See why I have no confidence in this model?" She then pointed to the number next to the line labeled "X coefficient" and shrieked, "Not only is the cost model unreliable, it says that overhead costs decrease as the number of cookies increases. How can that be?"

Sally examined the output and asked Debra how she could compute overhead cost when the equation related to the length of time required to produce a batch of cookies. Debra derived overhead costs as follows:

Overhead cost = $0.05 × (minutes per batch)

where

Minutes per batch = 26.476 − 0.448 × (number of cookies per batch)

Debra then multiplied the two lines together to get the following cost formula:

Overhead cost ($) = 0.53 − 0.02 × (number of cookies per batch)

Sally, after she had had a few minutes to examine the regression output and formula, said, "While I may have been absent the day my professor taught regression, I do remember there are other techniques we can use to estimate costs." She then requested, "Debra, show me the data!" Debra ran to her office, turned on her computer, accessed her spreadsheet file, printed a copy of the file, ran back to Sally's office, and presented her with the spreadsheet that appears on the next page.

Sally asked Debra if she thought the most recent estimates of $0.30 and $0.12 for direct material and direct labor costs per cookie, respectively, were reliable. Debra said the estimates were good approximations and should be used for all types of cookies. She continued, "I've always assumed that overhead explains the variation in cost per cookie. However, I'm really starting to question that assumption now." Sally thanked Debra and asked if she could meet with her in the next couple of days.

Discussion Questions

1. Use the following methods to produce an estimate of total cost per cookie. Apply these techniques using only one independent variable at a time. Use all independent variables provided above.
   - High-low method
   - Scatterplot method
   - Method of least squares

2. Using multiple regression, select the equation that produces the most accurate estimate of batch time.

3. What effect does your solution to question 2 have on CookieWorld's pricing decisions? Product mix decision? Process redesign?

2000 Cost Estimation Data for Various Types of Cookies

Batch	Minutes per Batch[1]	Number of Ingredients per Cookie[2]	Number of Processes per Batch[3]	Number of Cookies per Batch[4]
1	10	6	5	20
2	12	6	5	20
3	25	10	11	15
4	14	8	6	15
5	17	8	8	15
6	19	8	11	20
7	8	12	5	20
8	30	8	12	15
9	24	10	10	20
10	26	10	11	15
11	22	14	9	15
12	18	10	8	20
13	15	8	7	15
14	15	8	7	15
15	17	10	8	20
16	23	12	11	20
17	24	10	10	12
18	12	8	5	15
19	11	6	6	15
20	19	10	8	20
21	20	10	9	12
22	27	8	12	20
23	26	10	12	15
24	18	10	9	15
25	17	10	11	12
26	16	8	8	15
27	15	8	7	20
28	10	6	5	20
29	29	12	12	12
30	23	10	10	20
31	22	8	11	15
32	21	10	10	15
33	20	12	9	12
34	19	10	9	15
35	23	10	11	20

[1]This represents the time it takes to prepare ingredients for baking (from scratch up to the point of, but not including, baking).

[2] Examples of ingredients are flour, sugar, eggs, and lemon.

[3] Beating, grating, mixing, cutting, folding, and pouring are separate processes.

[4] This represents the number of cookies per pan.

Chapter 4

Activity-Based Costing (ABC)

Calculating Unit Costs Using ABC

Case 4.1

Part 1 or Part 2?

Joe Norton and his wife Lileth left their jobs in order to form their own company, Norton Industries, that manufactured two components of laptop computers. The two parts (hereinafter referred to as Part 1 and Part 2) were designed, manufactured, and sold separately.

For the last five years, Norton produced, on average, 25,000 units of Part 1 and 5,000 units of Part 2 (a unit equals one part). While the accounting records showed that both products were generating profits, Lileth's instincts told her otherwise.

Lileth Norton acted as the firm's chief financial officer and controller. She produced the accounting reports for the 10-person firm. She had the chance to observe their design and production practices on a daily basis and began to believe that Part 2 was much more costly to produce than Part 1. She talked to Joe about her belief, and he replied, "Lileth, the firm is profitable. Let's leave well enough alone. If it ain't broke, don't fix it."

Lileth responded, "Joe, I really feel something is wrong here, and I am going to take action." Over the next several weeks, Lileth pored over the inventory reports, parts of which are reproduced here.

Norton Industries
Cost per Part

		Part #1	Part #2
Parts produced		25,000	5,000
Volume characteristic		High	Low

Per part

		Part #1	Part #2
Direct material		$ 10.00	$ 10.00
Direct labor	$10.00 per hour		
Part #1	0.5 hours per part	5.00	
Part #2	0.5 hours per part		5.00

Manufacturing overhead
Machine overhead (maintenance, taxes, utilities)—unit level

		Part #1	Part #2
Machine cost	$40.00 per hour		
Part #1	2 hours	80.00	
Part #2	1 hours		40.00

Other overhead

		Part #1	Part #2
Budgeted overhead costs	$1,500,000.00		
Budgeted direct labor			
(Part #1 × [hours / part 1]) +			
(Parts 2 × [hours / part 2])	÷ 15,000.00		
Manufacturing overhead rate	$ 100.00 per DLH	50.00	50.00

	Part #1	Part #2
Total cost per part (DM+DL+MOH [MACHINE + OTHER])	**$145.00**	**$105.00**

Lileth also looked over the following data:

Activities and Costs	Budgeted Cost Pool	Budgeted Quantity
Engineering/design	$ 200,000	4,000 hours
Scheduling/planning	600,000	2,000 orders
Setups	500,000	2,000 set-ups
Inspection	200,000	4,000 inspections
	$1,500,000	

Activities Consumed	Part 1	Part 2
Engineering/design (number of hours)	1,000	3,000
Scheduling/planning (number of orders)	250	1,750
Setups (number of setups)	500	1,500
Inspections (number of inspections)	1,000	3,000

The more Lileth analyzed the data, the more confused she became.

Discussion Questions

1. If you were a consultant to this firm, what would you recommend? Assume the firm charges $150 per unit for Part 1 and $150 per unit for Part 2.

2. Assume Part 1 and Part 2 consume equal amounts of engineering, design, scheduling, planning, setup, and inspection resources. Would your recommendation change?

3. Assume the information in question 2, but add that the aforementioned activities are consumed in proportion to the number of units manufactured.

Case 4.2

Managed Care Consulting Services

Anne waited at home for the call that would send her on another consulting mission. Her home base was in New Orleans, but she flew all over the United States in order to apply her financial expertise. She specialized in health care. Specifically, she was hired to reengineer hospital patient care services.

Anne Gunner was born and raised in the Midwest. She attended a large state university in Iowa and received her master's degree in nursing. After 10 years of arduous (and truly devoted) nursing work, she felt burned out. Anne had always had a wide variety of interests, so at the end of her nursing career, she decided to go back to school to earn a master of business administration (MBA) degree.

When she completed the degree, she took a job with a nationally known health care consulting firm. Then, after five years with the firm, she decided to hang out her own shingle.

Anne really enjoyed cost accounting. Whenever she learned that a hospital used traditional cost accounting techniques and had not implemented an activity-based cost accounting/management system, she was excited because she felt she could provide value-added services to the organization.

Late one night, she received a call from Ted Sellon, a hospital administrator who said he needed help badly. His hospital had hired a marketing firm that, after reviewing the hospital's financial records, advised devoting many advertising dollars to promoting outpatient cosmetic surgery. The president of the marketing firm believed that the current low demand for such could be increased by double within a year.

Ted thought the plan would lead to the hospital's demise because the outpatient facility had a limited capacity. If cosmetic surgery services increased, then the other services, which involved sports medicine, would have to decrease. (The hospital had no way to add capacity in either area, so if one type of service increased, the other had to decrease.) Ted said that although the records did show that per-patient profits for sports medicine and cosmetic surgery were about the same, his intuition told him it wasn't so. Anne told Ted to fax her the most recent cost report, and she would start working on the case immediately. The report follows:

Hospital
Cost Report

			Sports Medicine (Patient #1)	Cosmetic Surgery (Patient #2)
Patients			500	100
Volume characteristic			High	Low
Per patient				
Direct material			$ 5	$ 5
Direct labor	$20.00 per hour			
Patient #1	5 hours per patient		100	
Patient #2	5 hours per patient			100
General hospital overhead				
Facility overhead (maintenance and utilities)--unit level				
Facility cost	$15.00 per hour			
Patient #1	1 hours		15	
Patient #2	2 hours			30
Other overhead				
Budgeted care overhead costs	$1,200,000			
Budgeted direct labor				
(Patient #1 × [hours / patient 1]) +				
(Patient #2 × [hours / patient 2])	÷ 3,000			
Care overhead rate	$ 400.00 per DLH		2,000	2,000
Total cost per patient (facility + other)			**$2,120**	**$2,135**

Ted also provided Anne with the following data:

Cost per Activity	Budgeted Cost Pool	Budgeted Total Quantity
Supporting service (number of hours)	$ 300,000	5,000
Capacity (number of peak hours)	200,000	1,000
Property taxes (square feet)	100,000	10,000
Exports (number of experts)	600,000	10
	$1,200,000	

Consumption	Sports Medicine	Cosmetic Surgery
Supporting services (number of hours)	3,000	2,000
Capacity (number of peak hours)	250	750
Property taxes (square feet)	5,000	5,000
Experts (number of experts)	2	8

Discussion Questions

1. Do you agree with the strategy recommended by the marketing firm about increasing cosmetic surgeries? Give calculations that support your conclusion. Assume the hospital recovers, on average, $3,000 per patient for both sports medicine and cosmetic surgery services.

2. Should hospitals eliminate all unprofitable services? What if the hospital were the only service provider in town and it discovered that its emergency room was unprofitable?

3. Should this ABC model be applied to a psychiatric center?

Case 4.3

ADT Uniforms: Part I

ADT Uniforms, Inc., located in Diablo Ridge, California, designs, manufactures, and markets apparel worn by employees in the food and beverage industry. ADT's strategy is to sell low-cost, high-quality uniforms to major franchise restaurants such as McDonald's, Pizza Hut, and Kentucky Fried Chicken.

ADT is known for producing a comfortable, polyester–cotton–blend garment that holds up in greasy and smoky environments. In fact, the uniforms are so comfortable that employees have been seen wearing them during off-hours. One of the shirts, the Rugger, is so popular that company chairman Harlan Stricker is considering approaching retail clothing stores in the hope of mass-marketing it under other brand names.

ADT's competitors produce similar products and price their goods competitively. However, they have not been able to duplicate the "touch and feel" of ADT's uniforms.

Though business has been brisk, Harlan believes the company should not be complacent. He has told his management team that he hopes to double sales and profits during the next two years. In order to achieve his goal, he put Sara Strap in charge of marketing. Sara decided that, instead of relying on established relationships and repeat business, she would require her sales force to hit the pavement and visit at least 10 franchise restaurants per week.

Sara began developing a special training program for the sales staff by identifying the most important topics in the general training manual.

Table of Contents

Chapter	Topic
1	Introduction
2	Demographics
3	Dress for Success
4	Greeting and Getting to Know the Customer
5	Bidding
6	Sealing the Deal
7	Contracts and Service

Sara felt she could develop most of the materials for the new manual herself, but she did not feel confident about the fifth chapter on bidding. When she was on the sales force, she was given fixed bid prices based on the uniform size, order quantity, and uniform type. She decided to change this procedure in order to give her sales staff some flexibility. Sara called ADT's controller, Tim Sanders, for more information about the issue.

The next day, the two met in the company cafeteria and discussed the activity-based costing (ABC) model that Tim used in budgeting, costing, and performance evaluation. After about an hour, Sara told Tim that she would like to use the ABC model to help her sales reps during the bidding process. She felt this would provide them with a competitive advantage.

Tim went back to his office, sat in front of his computer, and developed the Job Bid Sheet (which appears at the end of this case study). The job sheet contained standard cost data and cost drivers. In addition, Tim's office would collect actual cost data and evaluate manufacturing performance. The bidding portion of the sheet would be given to the sales force in Excel spreadsheet form. The reps had laptops and could plug in the appropriate amounts based on the customer's order and come up with a reasonable bid within seconds.

Tim sent the spreadsheet to Sara. She liked what she saw and required that each member of the sales force became proficient in using it. She also told her staff to forward a completed sheet to Tim on all successful bids.

Discussion Questions

1. What is the total cost to produce 1,000 uniforms? What is the unit cost per uniform?

2. Assuming a 40 percent markup in cost, what is the bid price for 1,000 uniforms? What is the unit bid price?

3. What items (including processes) could be changed to lower production costs?

ADT Uniforms Job Bid Sheet		
Bid number	J1103	
Customer	**Burger King**	
Product	Uniform	
Design number	W-103	
Number of units	1,000	
Standard Cost Data		
Direct Materials	**Quantity (Yards)/Uniform**	**Price/Yard**
Cotton cloth	2	$2.50
Polyester	4	$1.50
Direct Labor	**Hours/Uniform**	**Rate/Hour**
Cutting	0.75	$8.00
Sewing	1	$12.00
Overhead	**Cost Driver/Uniform**	**Rate/Cost Driver**
Washing		
Machine minutes	8	$0.20
Drying		
Machine minutes	10	$0.25
Folding		
Labor hours	0.05	$8.00
Actual Cost Data		
	Actual Cost	
Materials	$12,000.00	
Labor	17,000.00	
Overhead	5,000.00	
Bidding (Price) Information		
Price =		
Cost + Markup on DM+DL+ MOH		
Markup (%)	40%	

Case 4.4

ADT Uniforms: Part II

The ADT Uniforms, Inc., sales force was in the third month of its new "hit the pavement" sales campaign. ADT was continuing to show strong sales, but the feedback management received during a recent quarterly meeting caused them great concern. They were told that ADT's prices were higher than its competitors' when

- volume was high;
- the design was relatively simple; and
- only one or two sizes were offered.

ADT's bids were lower than its competitors' when

- volume was low;
- the design was complicated; and
- several different sizes were available.

In addition, Sara received a call from Tim, who told her that while sales continued to grow, profit margins were falling. Tim broke the news to Sara by saying, "We are going to have to train your staff to use a new ABC model."

Discussion Questions

1. What factors could explain the high and low bids?

2. What factors could explain the eroding profit margins?

3. Should ADT change the model? If so, how?

Chapter 5

ABC and ABM

Case 5.1

Bread Company: Part I

Allan Lloyd's best pitch was a fastball. In fact, his fastball will eventually get him inducted into the National Baseball Hall of Fame. Allan played for the Chicago Gray Sox for 15 years, and he won the MVP award twice. He won 20 or more games for six consecutive seasons. Many believe he was the reason the Gray Sox won the World Series.

Allan retired with a great reputation, health, and wealth. Sources close to him estimated his net worth to be around $60 million. Other than baseball, Allan didn't have many interests except for food. He loved to cook and bake, and he was especially good at baking bread. When automatic bread machines were introduced into the market, Allan responded by saying, "Automatic bread machines? What makes bread so good is a little tender, loving care. If you remove the human element, bread is no longer bread—it is just another carbohydrate."

Local socialite Betty Cape heard through the grapevine that Allan had strong feelings about bread and other foods. One night she spotted him at a party and approached him with an idea of starting a restaurant and café that featured exceptional bread. Allan was so excited about the idea that he wanted to start immediately. He told Betty he would call his friend and ex-teammate, Frank Smith, who was an accountant and his business advisor.

The following morning, Allan called Frank and asked how he could obtain cost information relating to the production of bread. Frank told him he would research the issue and provide him with a report in about two weeks. Allan thanked Frank and said he was most interested in baking and selling biscuits, muffins, and rolls at his restaurant.

Within a week, Frank called Allan and said, "Allan, a member of my accounting staff has begun to create a database of bread costs. It's amazing! When can I show it to you?" Allan responded, "Bring it over as soon as you can. I really want to sink my teeth into it."

The cost data, which were derived from Allrecipes.com and entered into an Access database (Access database file is provided on the enclosed disk), was broken down into the following categories:

Biscuits
Bread machine
Challah
Cornbread
Foccacia
Fruit bread
Grain bread
Herb bread
International
Breads
Muffins
Potato bread
Quick bread
Rolls
Wheat bread
White bread

The database also contained the following recipes:

Biscuits

Angel biscuit rolls
Angel biscuits
Angel biscuits II
Beaten biscuits
Beer biscuits
Blueberry monkey bread
Buttered biscuits
Cheddar biscuits
Cheese biscuits
Cinnamon buns
Cinnamon-sour cream biscuits
Easy biscuits
Fake sourdough biscuits
J. P.'s Big Daddy biscuits
Jam-filled buns
Lefse
Mom's baking powder biscuits
Monkey bread
Monkey bread II
Monkey bread III
Monkey bread IV
Monkey bread V
Red Lobster garlic cheese biscuits
Red pepper biscuits
Red pepper biscuits II
Sour cream biscuits
Sourdough drop biscuits
Taralli
Tarradls (Italian pepper rings)
Tea biscuits

Muffins

Alienated blueberry muffins
Apple bran cheddar muffins
Apple muffins
Banana chip muffins
Banana chip muffins II
Banana oat muffins
Banana-nut muffins
Best-ever muffins
Blueberry muffins
Bran muffins
Breakfast muffins

Rolls

Almond crescent buns
Butterscotch buns
Julia's hot cross buns
Croissants

Pecan sticky buns
Sticky buns
Tasty buns

Allan again thanked Frank for the information and told him he would get back to him as soon as possible.

Discussion Questions

1. List activities used to produce biscuits, muffins, and rolls.

2. Which activities could be redesigned and/or eliminated in order to reduce costs, yet at the same time maintain quality?

3. List significant cost drivers.

Case 5.2

Bread Company: Part II

After looking at the bread manufacturing cost data for several days, Allan Lloyd called Frank Smith hoping to learn more about the cost of producing a wide variety of high-quality biscuits, muffins and rolls. Allan knew how to make bread in his own kitchen, but the business side of the transaction was still a mystery. Allan told Frank that he had discovered 19 different processes in production. He provided Frank with the following list:

1. Mixing
2. Stirring
3. Storing
4. Kneading
5. Shaping
6. Cutting
7. Short baking
8. Medium baking
9. Long baking
10. Long rise
11. Boiling
12. Brushing
13. Beating
14. Cooling
15. Rolling
16. Drizzling, sprinkling
17. Half-hour baking
18. Dropping
19. Short rise

Then he showed Frank this list of possible ingredients.

Flour
Sugar
Baking powder
Baking soda
Salt
Shortening
Dry yeast
Water
Buttermilk
Salted butter
Low-gluten white flour
Chilled lard
Light cream
Beer
Dry frozen blueberries
Margarine
Vanilla extract
Ground cinnamon
Self-rising flour
Biscuit mix
Shredded cheddar cheese
Milk
Garlic powder
Dried parsley flakes
Parmesan cheese
Baking mix
Egg
Confectioners sugar
Brown sugar
Sour cream
Raisins
Sour milk
Light corn syrup
Cardamom
Chopped pecans
Ground nutmeg
Ground cloves
Onion powder
Crushed dried red pepper
Sourdough starter
Vegetable oil
Fennel seeds
Olive oil
Ground black pepper
Almonds
Blueberries
Wheat bran cereal
Baked apples
Whole wheat flour

Honey
Semisweet chocolate chips
Mashed bananas
Applesauce
Rolled oats
Chopped walnuts
Raisin bran cereal
All-Bran® cereal
Fresh fruit
Almond extract
Other chopped nuts
Orange peel
Lemon peel

After Frank read the list, Allan said, "Frank, how much does it cost to make bread?

Discussion Questions

1. Using the Access database, develop a cost model for making biscuits, muffins, and/or rolls.

2. Select one product and plug the relevant amounts into the equation you derived in question 1. How much does it cost to make the item you selected?

Chapter 6

Job-Order Costing

Case 6.1

Hollywood Parts, Inc.

Hollywood Parts, Inc., (HPI), is a plastic parts manufacturer in southern California. It is one of eight companies in the region that supply filmmakers with unique plastic pieces that are used to make characters and objects that appear on the big screen. HPI has established itself as one of the premier specialty-plastic shops because it has the shortest design-to-delivery time in the business.

HPI's founders and current owners, Dillan and Barbara Mills, are old-time-Hollywood movie junkies who have worked in the business for decades. At 18, Dillan was hired by one of the major film studios as a grip and worked his way up to production assistant. In this capacity, Dillan did everything from assisting in budget preparation to constructing movie sets. He really enjoyed the latter activity. Barbara started as a cartoonist but later became involved in the design and production of movie sets— which is where she was introduced to Dillan.

Soon after they met, Dillan and Barbara began dating and made every effort to be assigned to the same projects. They often worked together on movies involving science fiction creatures and outer-space adventures. These types of movies required specialty plastic parts and objects that had to be manufactured from scratch. Dillan and Barbara teamed up to design and produce these items with Barbara doing the creative/design work and Dillan the construction.

After seven years of marriage, the couple decided they would like to work more independently, so they quit their jobs at the studios and formed HPI. Having already established themselves in the business, they had no trouble receiving monetary support from local financial institutions.

On average, HPI bid on 10 jobs a week. The order quantities ranged from 10 to 500 parts, and the average order was for 50 parts. Dillan did the machining, and Barbara performed the necessary labor, which included designing and painting the product.

Dillan developed a bid from a process sheet that listed the activities required to make the final product. In some cases, material was provided by the customers; when it was not, Dillan purchased raw material and billed the client. Machine hours were billed out at a rate of $45 per hour, while the hourly billing rate for labor was $60. The final bid was based on the aforementioned rates. He added 25 percent for rush orders.

At the beginning, HPI was very successful. The company's early success was mostly due to Dillan and Barbara's reputation and business contacts. However, the couple noticed over time that profit margins were declining. In fact, although HPI continued to win 50 percent of its bids, Dillan believed the firm was losing money on some jobs. Dillan and Barbara called in an outside consultant, Howard Cargill, to help them uncover the problem. Howard asked for job-cost information for HPI's most recent jobs, and Dillan provided him with following list:

Job #1279

Raw material purchases	$15,000
Direct materials used	$12,000
Direct labor hours	40
Machine hours	20
Sales quote	$20,000
Beginning raw materials	0
Beginning work in progress	0
Beginning finished goods	0

Dillan also gave Howard a copy of the job sheet:

Order number	650	Job	1279
Part number	72c	Sales units	40

Date	Name	Hours
1/17	Barb M	6
1/19	Barb M	8
1/21	Barb M	2
	Ed T[1]	10
1/22	Barb M	4
	Ed T	10
	Total	**40**

[1] Ed Traylor (Ed T) was Barbara's assistant.

Discussion Questions

1. Should the firm use job-order or process accounting?

2. With respect to your answer to question 1, what process features did you decide are attributable to the accounting method you selected?

3. List possible reasons for HPI's falling margins.

Job Costing in an Accounting Firm

Case 6.2

Taxes in Texas

Blakely & Hudson, a large public accounting firm, specializes in tax planning and compliance. Its Houston office grew from a 10-person tax-professional operation to one containing more than 200 lawyers and accountants. The Houston office's big gun was Ross Forbes, who focused on oil and gas issues as well as estate- and gift-tax accounting. While Ross brought in the business, many felt Deborah Gandy was responsible for the firm's success.

Deborah was the partner in charge of day-to-day operations. Recently, she had heard rumors that employees were being forced to work many hours and were told not to bill all the time to the clients. When she asked her staff about it, they told her that the firm's managers were putting a ceiling on the number of hours that could be billed. They also said they were under intense pressure to complete jobs on time and in perfect working order.

Shocked by their revelation, Deborah decided to investigate the situation further. She started by listing the activities involved in the tax-preparation process. She came up with the following list and estimates of number of hours required by staff, managers, and partners.

		Staff	Manager	Partner
Step 1	**Client Identification and Acquisition**	0	0	10
	Client and partner agree on the nature of the job. A contract for services is signed.			
Step 2	**Financial Planning Questionnaire**	0	2	1
	Partner and manager discuss the job. Client is mailed a questionnaire.			
Step 3	**Year-End Tax Planning**	10	3	0
	Cash-flow and tax-minimization strategies are formulated and implemented.			
Step 4	**Tax Information Obtained from Client**	1	4	0
	Client and manager meet to discuss the tax return. Manager obtains information from client and gives it to staff.			
Step 5	**Tax Return Preparation**	15	3	0
	Staff prepares the return. Manager reviews the return.			
Step 6	**Tax Return Signoff**	4	2	0
	Manager and partner agree that the return is complete and accurate. Tax return is given to client and/or an extension is filed.			
Step 7	**Partner and Client Follow-Up**	0	1	4
	Partner communicates with client regarding tax return and future tax planning engagements.			

Deborah also obtained the following rate structure:

Average Hourly Rate

Staff	$ 90
Managers	$150
Partners	$300

She discovered that, on average, clients were charged $5,000 per return (this amount included fees for year-end tax planning).

After performing the relatively simple calculations relating to the job, she cried, "No wonder staff are not reporting all their hours. If they did, these jobs would be big losers!"

Discussion Questions

1. On average, what is the profit (loss) per job?

2. Should the following costs be assigned to the job?
   - Client identification and acquisition
   - Overhead
   - Supplies
   - Idle time
   - Training

3. Since tax return preparation is a relatively homogenous process, is a job-order accounting system appropriate in these circumstances?

Chapter 7

Process Costing

Case 7.1

Logo Cup, Inc.

Logo Cup, Inc., (LCI), designs, produces, and sells specialty plastic cups. LCI produces nonstandard plain cups, attaches a logo to a standard cup, or attaches a logo to a specially-designed cup. The order quantities range from 25 to 20,000 cups. Most orders are in the 10,000 to 20,000 range.

The production process is process-oriented. The factory consists of five areas devoted to plastic forming and molding, painting, assembly, quality control, and packaging. Employees specialize in their respective areas and receive no training in the other areas. Their job is repetitive for the most part.

The production process can best be explained by way of illustration. Assume the firm receives an order for 10,000 mugs that will have a professional sports logo on the outside. When the production supervisor receives the order, he or she sends a message to each of the departments so that the department supervisors can do their own planning. The production supervisor then orders the plastic resin (if necessary) for the job.

The design is placed in a mold, that can make 10 to 12 cups at a time. In addition, the forming and molding department produces the handles for the mugs. The cups are placed in bins that hold 500 cups or handles. The bins move to the printing department only when the order is completed or the bin is full.

The painting department places the logo on the mug and sends the mug and handle to assembly once the bin is full. Assembly connects the handle and mug before the quality-control department inspects the final product. The average defect rate is about 3 percent. After the mugs pass inspection, they are packaged and sent to the shipping docks.

Mary Wittingham, LCI's CEO, is concerned about the firm's ability to fill small orders and its ever-increasing inventory. On a recent plant trip, she noticed that full bins were piled high throughout the factory.

She called the production supervisor, Andrew Meister, and asked him about the feasibility of using cellular manufacturing techniques. Cellular manufacturing differs from the traditional methods in that each cell has a team of cross-trained workers who produce a specific product such as mugs or plastic cups. Andrew believed cellular manufacturing had potential and suggested they set up a pilot test before changing the entire factory operation.

Andrew asked for volunteers who would be trained in each of the production areas. The cell would be a microcosm of the factory floor, with each member focusing on his or her own designated function. In the event one person in the cell experienced a problem, the other cell members could help solve it since they had received training in all areas of production, too.

Mary asked Andrew to provide some information regarding the cell's performance after the group had been working for a month. The information presented in Andrew's report follows.

Logo Cup, Inc.

	Traditional	Cellular
Defect rate	3%	1%
Throughput time (days)	4	1
Throughput time (minutes)	1920	480
Output rate (units/day)	2,500	2,500
Number of units per bin	500	500
Labor content (min./unit)	3	3
Labor content (min./day)	7,500	7,500
Processing time (min./unit)	1	1
Workers	40	40
Hours per day	8	8
Available labor time (min./day)	19,200	19,200
Machine time used (min./unit)	4	4
Machine time used (min./day)	10,000	10,000
Machines	25	35
Machine time available	12,000	16,800

Discussion Questions

1. Write a memo to Mary that explains how the cellular manufacturing system influenced the operations of Logo Cup, Inc.

2. In the memo, provide a table similar to the one below by filling in the missing performance measures. Discuss how the measures changed.

Performance Item	Performance Measure	Traditional Method	Cellular Manufacturing
Quality	Defect rate (%)		
Inventory level	Work-in-process inventory (# of cups)		
Throughput time	Factory cycle time (min./unit)		
Equipment productivity	Factory machine utilization (%)		
Labor productivity	Factory labor utilization (%)		

Case 7.2

---

eLicious.com

The Wall Street Gazette, Tuesday, July 10, 2000

> CEO Gulps as Profits Ripple
>
> Acacia, Ohio—eLicious.com announced that its second-quarter net income fell 5 percent from its previous year's mark. Harry Best, the firm's CEO, attributed the decrease to unpredictable demand and to what he referred to as "misinformation." Best vowed to increase sales by 10 percent and to implement new information systems that would provide a more accurate picture of the firm's costs.

After the press conference, Best asked to be driven immediately to headquarters. During the car trip, he asked his assistant, Paul Cameron, to read him the most recent mission statement and to call the firm's new accounting guru, Kellie Shea. He wanted to meet with Shea in his office as soon as he returned.

While driving down Interstate 71, Paul read Harry the firm's mission statement: "eLicious.com aims to become the premier online custom-beverage company in the United States. This will be accomplished by meeting the unique demands of every customer, by ensuring that a high-quality product is delivered to the customer within three days, and by providing a family-oriented, healthy product. This will enable the company to earn competitive returns for shareholders and to attract talented and loyal employees."

A couple of seconds after Paul finished, Harry said with a chuckle, "That sure is a mouthful!" He then asked Paul whether the company should mass-produce a few unique products or continue to allow customers to customize their own health drinks. Paul pointed out that about half of eLicious's customer base selects one of the standard drinks, while the other half chooses to customize. In addition, data revealed that more than 80 percent of all sales were made to customers who asked to have their names displayed on the beverage bottle. This cost an additional $0.50 per bottle.

As the two arrived at headquarters, Harry told Paul that he had a meeting with Kellie and thanked him for his efforts. When Harry arrived at his office, Kellie was waiting for him. Harry told Kellie that he thought the information regarding product costs was not accurate. He could not understand how costs for the standard and customized products were about the same. He asked her to prepare a report that would tell him the following:

1. How do the standard- and custom-product manufacturing processes differ?
2. Do the two procedures require different types of information?
3. To what extent do materials differ for the two products?
4. How different are the products?
5. How is performance evaluated?
6. What role does labor play in the two processes?
7. To what extent are processes related to the mission statement?

Kellie told Harry that she would complete the report in one week.

Discussion Question
Answer questions 1 through 7 above.

Chapter 8

Cost Allocation

Case 8.1

How Will Her Achilles Heal?

Volleyball was their passion. For the past 10 years, Shelley Fray and her friends reserved Tuesday night for volleyball. The group would meet at Shelley's apartment complex, which had the area's best sand-volleyball courts.

In the beginning, the group's skills were raw, but, as time progressed, they became pretty good, which caused the games to be competitive and fast-paced. Diving, digging, spiking, and taunting were all part of the games. The players enjoyed themselves so much that when winter came to the Chicago-area community, they investigated the possibility of moving indoors.

As it turned out, the answer was right under their noses: The complex had an indoor racquetball court that could be converted for volleyball. The indoor game, called walleyball, was different from the outdoor game in that the rules permitted players to hit balls off the walls. The walls were treated as part of the playing field.

One cold Tuesday night in December, nine players met. The game proceeded as usual until Shelley spiked the ball and hit Paul Green in the head. Paul didn't like being hit and vowed to return the favor. Shelley began playing cautiously and noticeably took a step back when the ball was hit near Paul. Fortunately, Paul and Shelley met between games and declared a truce.

After another game or two, Shelley began to relax and enjoy herself again. She began to joke and started taking unusual shots. She even dove on the hardwood floor in an effort to win points.

During the last game of the evening, the ball was hit over Shelley's head. She leaped for it and fell backwards. As she collected herself, she told the group she had heard a loud pop and asked whether one of the ceiling tiles had fallen. The group looked at the ceiling and found nothing missing. Shelley then began feeling pain in her left leg and couldn't stand up.

Her friends surrounded her and asked what had happened. She said she didn't know and asked to be driven to the hospital. She felt something was very wrong.

When Shelley arrived, her leg was examined and x-rayed. The doctor told Shelley she had torn her Achilles tendon and gave her two treatment options: surgery or prolonged rest. In either case, extensive rehab was required. Shelley opted for surgery, which took place the next day. She began rehab within a week.

Shelley could choose to come to the hospital for rehab or have a therapist visit her at home. She asked how much the in-hospital and the at-home treatments would cost. Dr. Carl Stanley, who was in charge of the sports medicine clinic, said both treatments cost about the same. Shelley took the at-home treatment. After she left the office, Dr. Stanley began thinking about the cost of the two treatments. He questioned whether costs should be the same for two different types of services. He called the hospital's controller, Judy Harris, and asked if they could meet for lunch and discuss the cost structure for the two treatments.

When they met, Judy showed Dr. Stanley the following table, which summarized cost information over the past year.

Cost Data—Achilles Tendon Rehabilitation

	Total	In-House	At-Home
Revenues			
Number of patients	60	20	40
Number of treatments	9,000	3,000	6,000
Total revenue	$135,000	$45,000	$90,000
Costs			
Supplies	$ 12,000	$ 7,000	$ 5,000
Equipment	30,000	10,000	20,000
Nursing services	45,000	15,000	30,000
General overhead	15,000	5,000	10,000
	$102,000	$37,000	$65,000
Profit	**$ 33,000**	**$ 8,000**	**$25,000**

She told him that, in the past, supply costs were the only costs that were traced to a particular treatment. All other costs were allocated using ratios involving recoverable amounts for each type of treatment to total recoverable amounts for both treatments.

Dr. Stanley looked over the numbers one more time and said, "My intuition is that since the treatment processes are different, the cost should be different as well." Judy agreed but told him that the hospital administration did not want to use activity-based cost accounting because it might not add value. Dr. Stanley said, "OK, but can we work on this? I mean, why don't we look into it in our own spare time, and, if our analysis tells us anything interesting, we can present it to the board."

Judy said, "As if we have spare time! But for you, Dr. Stanley, I will do it." Within two weeks, Judy prepared the following tables that would serve as a basis for their analysis.

Table I: Cost Allocation Methods

Traditional

Recoverable amount ratio = Recoverable amounts per treatment / Total amount recoverable

Activity-Based	In-House	At-Home
Square footage	1,000	150
Utility costs (kW/hr)	150,000	20,000
FTE (full-time equivalents)	6	1

Table II: General Overhead

	Total
Facility costs	$ 3,000
Utilities	2,000
Support staff (records)	10,000
Total	$15,000

Discussion Questions

1. What is the cost of providing in-house rehabilitation? At-home rehabilitation?

2. How do you think the hospital board will react to the analysis?

3. What other factors should the board consider in deciding what type of treatments it should provide?

4. How will (should) the information influence Dr. Stanley's behavior?

Case 8.2

Enable the Cable!

Joe loved to watch television. He set the TV's alarm so it awakened him in time for the first daily broadcast of ESPN SportsCenter. The television shuts off after the night's last Howard Stern show. If it were not for work, Joe would have watched television all day long.

Since TV was such a big part of Joe's life, he thought a job that would allow him to work at home would be perfect. If he could get what he called "one of those virtual-office-type jobs," he would be set for life. He could then work and watch television all the time.

While working as a computer programmer for J-Pro Associates, Joe received a call from a computer software company asking whether he would be interested in leaving his current position. He said he would but only if he could work at home. The company's human resources specialist said that the new firm wouldn't mind as long as Joe sent in coding (computer code) at the end of each day. Joe interviewed and got the job.

Joe lived in a two-bedroom apartment on the west side of Beverly, Idaho. The apartment had three cable outlets; two outlets were in service. On the last day of his employment with J-Pro, Joe began thinking about how he would set up his home office. He began cleaning out the spare bedroom that night.

After three hours of cleaning and deep thought, Joe suddenly cried out, "Hey, hey! We have lift-off! He shoots, he scores!" He had just uncovered the third cable outlet. Joe called the local cable company the next morning and requested a sales representative. When the salesperson answered the phone, Joe said, "To whom am I talking?" The sales manager replied, "My name is Katy Hasslemen." Joe replied, "Well Katy, it's that time again—would you please 'enable the cable!?'"

Katy said, "What?" Joe clarified, "Would you please turn on the third cable outlet in my apartment?" Katy responded, "Yes, but it will take a couple of days. We'll be out on Wednesday." He replied, "Thank you, and how much will it be?"

She provided him with the following information.

One-Time Hookup	Hookup Price	Monthly Fee Increase
1. Outlet installed	$19.50	$0.00
2. No outlet (installation of outlet required, service must be turned on)	$39/hour	$0.00

Joe said, "I have an outlet—it just needs to be turned on. But I might want another one or two installed in my kitchen and on my patio deck." She said, "Well, just give us a call when you decide."

Discussion Questions

1. Explain the fee schedule.

2. Using activity-based costing concepts, explain the fee schedule.

3. How appropriate is the use of ABC in this context?

Chapter 9

Budgeting

Case 9.1

Spa-Go

Anne Bowlan was visiting her brother, George, in St. Louis, Missouri. He was a doctor who had a home in Kirkwood and an A-frame cottage on a lake about 90 minutes from his home. The brother and sister met there with their families for Thanksgiving dinner. It was a tradition that, after the meal, the families would convene to the spa located on the deck outside the living room. The spa was large, holding eight adults at a time.

Anne enjoyed the spa so much that she vowed to have Thanksgiving dinner (including her own newly installed spa, which she did not have at the time) the following year. That meant she had 12 months to buy the spa and get it up and running.

When she returned to her home in Indiana, she contacted friends in the area who also owned spas. They recommended that she waste no time and told her to start shopping as soon as possible. Three places in Anne's central Indiana community sold spas: Menard's, Lowe's, and Lyons Pool & Patio. She decided on the King Zebra model, which was sold only by Lyons. The list price was $6,000. However, if Anne purchased the King Zebra during Lyons' New Year's sale, she would receive a 20 percent discount plus a free cover and ladder.

The easy part was over. Purchasing the spa was no problem—anyone with time could do that. The difficult part was getting the spa installed. She concluded that the best contractor in the area was Gregg Pawlos, who told her that if she purchased the supplies, he would install the spa for $40 per hour. He gave her the following list of materials:

Concrete block	12" x 12" x 3" blocks, 36 blocks total
Sand for leveling	2 50-lb. bags
Fencing	6' x 6' fencing (6 units)
Fence posts	9' x 4" x 4" (2 posts)

She also contacted a local electrician, who suggested that she install a 220-volt line that would easily carry the power to the spa's heater and to its engine that generated the water massage. The bill from Bob's Electric would amount to $800.

After shopping for materials at Lowe's and Menard's, she discovered that prices were very similar. However, Menard's had a sale on concrete block.

She purchased the following items for the following amounts:

Concrete block, 12" x 8" x 3"	54 blocks	$1.00 per block
Sand, 50-lb. bags	2 bags	$10.00 per bag
Fencing, 6 x 6'	6 units	$50 per unit
Fence posts, 9' x 4" x 4"	2 posts	$8 per post

In less than one week, the materials arrived and were placed on the side lawn. It cost $0.05 per block, $0.10 per bag, $0.20 per fence unit, and $0.15 per post to unload the items from the truck.

Lyons required $1,000 down, which Anne paid by check when she finalized the purchase. The remainder would be due upon delivery.

As Anne sat and thought about her purchase, she began to think in terms of cash flow. In about one month all of her bills would be due.

Discussion Questions

1. Prepare a schedule that lists costs at various activity levels. Assume Gregg works 10, 15, 20, and 25 hours.

2. Classify the costs as direct material, direct labor, and overhead.

3. Gregg offered to purchase the materials and then charge material costs plus his hourly labor rate. Did Anne make a good decision to purchase the materials herself?

4. In the production process, is Anne a buyer, supplier, supervisor? Why is this arrangement acceptable?

Activity-Based Budgeting

Case 9.2

GoForma, Inc.

GoForma, Inc. (GFI) manufactures and distributes hair-care products ranging from baby shampoo to wash-and-rinse coloring products. Since the industry is extremely competitive, GFI does extensive market and financial analysis before it introduces a new product.

Telly Salvidores was, until recently, the designer/developer of a software package called Planware that was used to perform the type of financial analysis GFI does during new-product development. GFI thought Telly brought a competitive advantage because he was a capable analyst who could also custom-design the software package to meet the special needs of the company.

Telly and GFI's management worked well together for several years until Telly received an offer he could not refuse from a competing company, Irie Hair Products. The offer included a substantial raise, an attractive cash bonus package, and stock options. Stock ownership was something Telly always wanted. Unfortunately, GFI was owned by one woman who was reluctant to give up any ownership or control of the company. Telly and GFI had a friendly parting of the ways, but his departure left a big hole in the firm.

Telly couldn't have left at a worse time. GFI profits were declining during a period in which it had hoped to introduce a new product that would, according to GFI, leave its competitors in the dust. The firm really needed a financial analyst who understood the details of the hair-care business. To make matters even worse, when Telly left, so did the software. Telly and the firm had agreed in writing that if Telly left GFI, the software could no longer be used by anyone in the firm.

Valerie, the firm's owner, responded by calling a meeting of the accounting and finance departments. She told the employees that they would have to develop a software package similar to Telly's within a month. She further told them that she had a new product and would need some detailed financial analysis before she would begin producing and marketing it.

Valerie asked the group whether this was feasible. Warren, one of the new accountants on staff, said, "I am a former C++ and Visual Basic programmer. I can do it and will build a model I read about in the *Harvard Business Review* called 'Discovery Driven Planning'. However, I am going to need some information before I begin." Valerie responded by handing him a stack of computer printouts from Planware. Listed below is information derived from the printouts.

Current profits	$5,000,000
Target increase in profits	10%
Profit margin	30%
Target cost	70%
Unit sales price	$8.50
Order size (of bottles)	250
Calls required to make a sale	3
Calls per salesperson per day	20
Workdays	250
Salary per salesperson	$25,000
Production per hour (units per hour)	60
Productive hours per day per worker	8
Production days	250
Workers per line	7
Salary per line worker	$30,000
Material cost—direct material per unit	$3
Packaging cost per unit	$0.50
Containers per order	10
Cost per container	$0.45

Annual depreciation per product line	$6,000
Administrative salaries	$125,000
Administrative overhead	$50,000

Discussion Questions

1. Using the data provided, prepare a detailed financial analysis that includes an income statement.

2. Should GFI introduce the new product?

3. What if Valerie decides that the profit increase need be only 5 percent? How does this change your analysis decision?

4. How would your analysis be affected if sales and production salaries increased by 10 percent?

**Managerial Decision
Cases**

Chapter 10

Variance Analysis

Case 10.1

The Henson Brothers

Regional Sports Authority, Inc., (RSA), was the Midwest's premier producer of hockey pucks. RSA made a high-quality puck at a reasonable price. Most college and high school hockey teams used the RSA pro-line model.

The firm's headquarters was in Madison, Wisconsin, but the pucks were manufactured in Duluth, Minnesota. Duluth provided a rich source of experienced labor, and a local distributor sold RSA its raw materials.

Over the past five years, Duluth had experienced some of its coldest winters. December temperatures averaged −10 degrees Fahrenheit. This weather caused some local residents to move away to warmer climates. The flight from the north was so great, in fact, that several local merchants were also considering leaving the picturesque community.

The effects of the flight were felt by RSA. The skilled labor force was dwindling, and this drove up labor costs. CEO Chad Neumann became convinced that the increase in labor costs would significantly reduce profits. Chad wanted to know more about the firm's financial situation, so he called RSA's controller, Sheila Winsett, and asked her how the changing labor force was affecting productivity and efficiency.

Sheila informed Chad that profits had declined significantly over the past three years, but she went on to say that Tony, the HR director, had hired a "secret weapon"—three brothers who knew much about the puck production process. Tony hired the Henson brothers at a premium when they told him they would do whatever it took to beat the competition. Sheila learned that the Hensons had already started and that things looked promising. Chad asked her to prepare a production report that included variance analysis for the period since the brothers began working. When Sheila returned to her office to prepare the report, she discovered that her staff had already started analyzing the brothers' performance.

Listed below is information that Sheila found on her desk.

Units produced	100,000 pucks
Standard costs	
Direct materials	Per puck
Standard quantity	0.25 lb.
Standard price	$2.00/lb.
Direct labor	
Standard hours	0.15
Standard rate	$8.00 per hour
Variable overhead	
Standard hours	0.15
Standard rate	$6.00 per hour
Actual costs	
Actual quantity—purchases	30,000 lb.
Actual quantity—production	26,000 lb.
Actual price—purchases	$1.90 per lb.
Direct labor	
Actual hours	10,000
Actual rate	$10.00 per hour
Variable overhead	
Actual hours	10,000
Actual rate	$6.00 per hour

Discussion Questions

1. Analyze the Henson brothers' performance by calculating the direct material, direct labor, and variable overhead variances.

2. Was hiring the Hensons a good decision?

Case 10.2

Meleagris Gallopavo, Inc.

Meleagris Gallopavo, Inc., (MGI), is one of seven turkey producers throughout the world. Its production facility is in northern Iowa and employs about 700 people. It is a principal supplier to one of the United States' leading sellers of turkeys. The well-known seller buys the turkeys from MGI, injects them with a buttery mixture, and distributes and sells its product internationally.

MGI does not breed and raise turkeys. The firm buys live fowl from nearby farms and processes them into a form (whole turkey) that can be immediately cooked or processed further. It also cuts the turkey into pieces and produces other processed turkey products such as turkey burgers, turkey sausage, and turkey sandwich slices.

Recently, profits have been falling in the operating segment that produces whole turkey. Jackie Fern, the firm's CEO, was alarmed because Thanksgiving was just around the corner.

Jackie called in Tom Benz, the production manager. She told Tom that profits were "falling faster than a pig on ice skates." She said the firm's controller, Dawn Dean, had traced the problem to production. She understood that production costs were increasing but had not found the specific cause. Jackie asked Tom to work with Dawn to find it. Tom went immediately to Dawn's office, where he found her slumping over a cost report. Dawn looked up at Tom when he walked in and said, "Let's get to work." Dawn handed Tom the following report.

September Cost Report

Production: 3,900 whole turkeys

Sales: 3,900 whole turkeys

Standard costs

	Standard Price/ Rate	Standard Quantity/ Hours	Standard Cost per Unit
Direct materials	$0.50/lb.	10 lb.	$5.00
Direct labor	9.00/hr.	2/3 hr.	$6.00
Variable overhead	6.00/hr.	2/3 hr.	$4.00

Actual costs

Direct materials price	$0.45/lb.
Direct materials quantity	10 lb./turkey
Direct labor	$9.20/hr.
Total hours	3,300
Variable overhead—total	$20,000

Discussion Questions

1. Calculate the direct materials, direct labor, and variable overhead variances.

2. Prepare a table as follows:

Item	Amount (Favorable [F]/Unfavorable [U])
Materials price variance	
Materials quantity variance	
Labor rate variance	
Labor efficiency variance	
Variable overhead spending variance	
Variable overhead efficiency variance	

3. Explain the source of MGI's problem.

Case 10.3

Who Runs the Floor?

Julie and Ted Rossi joined the firm of Roscoe, Incorporated, a maker of top-of-the-line bicycles, two weeks after they were married. Although they had had a joyous wedding and a memorable honeymoon, they couldn't wait to start their new jobs. Ted started in production, Julie in accounting.

The couple had met in college, where they both entered the business administration program as freshmen, intending to major in operations and production management. However, after two years and a couple of accounting courses, Julie switched to accounting because she believed power within any organization was concentrated in the controller's office. After her sophomore year, she told Ted that "whoever runs the books runs the production floor." Ted disagreed and told her that production managers rule because they have more direct contact with the manufacturing process and employees.

Ted and Julie disagreed about little else. They finished college with very high grades and were perceived as the ideal couple. One of the reasons the two were so compatible was that they both loved mountain biking. On their honeymoon in Colorado, they scheduled bike rides seven days out of their ten-day stay. They even took their Roscoe Deluxe bicycles with them on their trip.

Their future employer produced a product that was their passion. So, naturally, Julie and Ted thought they would live and work in eternal bliss. In fact, Ted was so confident about his and the company's future that, when given the option of a flat $50,000 salary or a $20,000 salary plus a bonus that was tied to production, he chose the latter. Julie was concerned about this decision because she knew she could probably influence the amount of compensation he—and therefore they—would receive. Julie asked her supervisor, Bryan Hills, about it, and he told her not to worry since he made and was responsible for all decisions that would affect Ted's salary.

During the first year, Ted got off to a great start. He received a $45,000 bonus for his apparent ability to control overhead. Since the total fixed and variable overhead variance was favorable, he got $30,000. He was paid an additional $15,000 because actual production exceeded the budgeted amount.

The couple celebrated Ted's triumph at a local bar. Julie was happy because Ted was so excited. However, she was hiding her concern about a compensation system that was sensitive to the amounts set at the initial budget meeting. When they returned home from the bar, she asked Ted if he would switch to the flat salary plan if given the choice. He responded, "No way!" She decided not to push it.

The next day, Bryan asked Julie to gather data for next month's budget meeting. He specifically asked her to prepare a schedule that listed last year's overhead budget and actual activities and costs. Later that week, she gave him the following information.

Budgeted Amounts
(1999)

Overhead

Variable overhead	$2,000,000
Budgeted fixed overhead	$4,000,000
Denominator activity	20,000 direct labor hours
Budgeted units	10,000

Actual Results
(1999)

Overhead

Actual variable overhead	$2,500,000
Actual fixed overhead	$4,500,000
Actual activity	27,000 direct labor hours
Actual units produced	12,000

When she presented the data to Bryan, he said, "Let's budget the same amount for next year, except let's adjust the denominator activity. It looks like 30,000 is more like it. I mean, we are not going to be off by 7,000 hours again this year." She took note of his comment and returned to her office.

After the year ended, Julie looked at the actual production data with respect to overhead. She looked with great interest at the following report.

Actual Amounts
(2000)

Overhead

Actual variable overhead	$2,500,000
Actual fixed overhead	$4,500,000
Actual activity	27,000 direct labor hours
Actual units produced	10,000

Discussion Questions

1. Calculate the variable and fixed overhead variances for 1999 and 2000.

2. What should Julie tell Ted about his compensation for 2000?

3. Who runs the floor?

Chapter 11

Responsibility Accounting

Case 11.1

Earnings Surprise

Sometimes surprises can be good—and sometimes they can be bad. In this case, the surprise was bad. The current-period earnings picture was really bad. Profits appeared to have fallen like a bowling ball off a cliff. This was what the firm's controller, Marcus Shelley, told CEO Mimi Carol.

Mimi was shocked because she thought the firm's recent successes would continue for a long time. She was so convinced of it that she called in an outside accounting forensic specialist to recreate the firm's financial statements for the current and prior three-year periods.

Mimi met with Karl Hapel, an accounting professor from a local university who had written several papers about how books could be altered to portray a more positive financial picture. This case was different in that a CEO of a mid-sized manufacturing company believed someone either erred or altered the books to make the firm look as if it were in decline. Mimi also felt the current financial performance was so low that compensation for most of the top executives would be at least 50 percent lower than the prior year. All compensation packages for the top executives included a bonus that was triggered when net income exceeded the prior year's amounts, or $10,000,000.

Karl asked for a statement of amounts for the last four years. He told Mimi it would take him one week to line up a new set of financials. Mimi called Marcus immediately and asked him to bring what Karl had requested. In less than an hour, Marcus handed both Mimi and Karl a copy of the following accounts.

Schedule of Accounts
(000,000s)

Raw Material Warehouse

	1997	1998	1999	2000
Beginning raw materials inventory	$ 5,000	$ 2,000	$ 3,000	$ 5,000
Purchases of raw materials	15,000	20,000	25,000	20,000
Ending raw materials inventory	2,000	3,000	5,000	5,000

Factory

	1997	1998	1999	2000
Direct labor	$30,000	$43,000	$52,000	$45,000
Manufacturing overhead:				
Indirect materials	$ 1,000	$ 2,000	$ 2,500	$ 1,700
Indirect labor	4,000	5,000	3,000	4,500
Depreciation, factory	1,200	1,200	1,200	1,200
Property taxes, factory	800	800	800	800
Utilities, factory	1,500	1,600	2,000	1,800
Insurance, factory	550	550	550	550
Beginning work-in-process	$ 7,500	$ 5,500	$ 2,500	$ 4,000
Ending work-in-process	$ 5,500	$ 2,500	$ 4,000	$ 2,000

Finished Goods Warehouse

	1997	1998	1999	2000
Beginning finished goods	$ 10,000	$ 12,000	$ 15,000	$ 8,000
Ending finished goods	12,000	15,000	8,000	6,000

Headquarters

	1997	1998	1999	2000
Selling expenses	$ 12,000	$ 14,000	$ 16,000	$ 14,000
Administrative expenses	20,000	22,000	24,000	25,000

Income Statement

	1997	1998	1999	2000
Sales	$100,000	$120,000	$150,000	$120,000

Discussion Questions

1. What is net income for the years 1997 to 2000?

2. Why did net income drop so dramatically in 2000?

Case 11.2

Leb, Inc.

Leb, Inc., (Leb), was one of the leading tie manufacturers in the world. Leb sold to high-end retailers in Paris, Tokyo, Milan, New York, and Chicago. The firm was known for its classic, fashionable designs and for its superb materials and manufacturing.

A decade ago, Leb diversified its operations by purchasing a small company that produced and sold tie clasps and cuff links. Leb's management thought the firm could distribute and sell its new product line at the same retail locales.

After several years of success, CEO Merle Gill noticed that, while tie sales fluctuated with seasons and trends, tie clasps and cuff link sales remained relatively constant. So, at certain times of the year, or during certain years, Leb's tie inventory could be very high or nonexistent.

The inventory situation concerned Merle; he thought the firm should do a better job of predicting and meeting demand. He told his production manager, Mary Page, "The next time I see a warehouse full of ties, someone is going to be fired."

Merle also had other problems. Due to high inventory and labor problems, the firm's profits were shrinking. His highly skilled employees were becoming discontented because their schedule was unpredictable. They wanted a steady, 40-hour week as opposed to workloads that ranged from 20 to 65 hours per week.

The declining margins could also be explained by increasing competition, especially in Paris. France's leading hosiery manufacturer, Lambert, Inc., shifted its focus from hosiery to ties and suits. The French firm's new line of ties was very popular in Europe and in the United States. Unfortunately, Leb's manufacturing operations were not flexible enough to meet the shift in demand caused by Lambert.

Merle decided to take action. He learned that Lambert, Inc., had not only new products, but also a new performance measurement system called *tableau de borde*. Several U.S. companies were designing and implementing similar systems that were referred to as *balanced scorecards*. Merle thought such a system would help his company, and he assigned the task of designing the scorecard to his top managers.

Merle asked his secretary to type and send the following memo:

> **Urgent!** Your assistance is needed now. Please make plans to meet me at headquarters on December 15. You must design a balanced scorecard for Leb, Inc. I will ask you to present your scorecard at the meeting. Each of you will have a half-hour to make your presentation. After the presentations are finished, we will decide what will best suit our firm's needs.

The message was sent to the firm's vice presidents of sales and marketing, manufacturing, finance, and human resources. In addition, Merle asked Leb's strategic planning group to develop a scorecard that would be presented at the meeting.

When the group met, the tension was obvious. Each vice president wanted to make sure that he or she would benefit from (and, more important, not be hurt by) the new measurement system.

Discussion Questions

1. Develop a balanced scorecard for Leb, Inc. (a blank scorecard is provided on the next page).

2. How would each vice president's scorecard differ?

3. Is a balanced scorecard approach appropriate for Leb?

Balanced Scorecard
Leb, Inc.

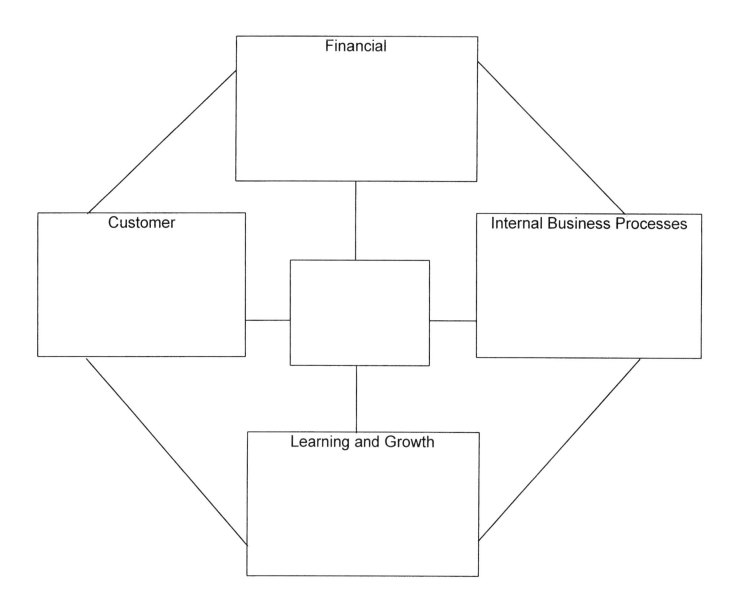

Chapter 12

Performance Evaluation

Case 12.1

CAT versus Komatsu

Caterpillar, Inc.

(The content of this section is derived from http://www.caterpillar.com.)

This Peoria, Illinois, company is a leader in producing construction, mining, and agricultural equipment. Caterpillar's machines play a critical role in developing the world's mining, harvesting, transportation, and housing systems. Its 200 dealers reach an equal number of countries worldwide.

The company also produces engines for boats and trucks; generators for drilling rigs, mines, and small communities; and energy supplies for hospitals and airports. In addition, it provides logistic, insurance, and financial services. Sales of the "CAT" clothing line exceed $200 million annually.

The company's founders, Benjamin Holt and Daniel Best, each developed heavy-duty tractors around the turn of the twentieth century, but later joined forces to form the Caterpillar Tractor Co. Some of the company's early growth can be linked to the use of its products in both world wars. In World War II, Caterpillar developed products that were used in the United States' tank arsenal.

It wasn't until 1950, though, that the firm began to have offices overseas. In the early 1960s, it joined forces with Mitsubishi and has since become a big player in Japanese markets. In 1998, Caterpillar's sales and profits exceeded $20 billion and $2 billion, respectively. With respect to revenue, it was the firm's best year ever. Profits fell just short of its record profits of a year earlier.

After its financial successes in 1997 and 1998, the firm had some good and bad news. On the upside, Caterpillar received the Malcom Baldridge United States National Quality Award. On the downside, the firm's highly respected chairman, Donald Fites, announced his retirement.

See page 104 for selected financial information for Caterpillar for the period 1977 to 1995.

Komatsu, Ltd.

(The content of this section is derived from http://www.komatsu.com.)

Komatsu Ltd., headquartered in Tokyo, Japan, manufactures and markets a wide variety of products and services ranging from its principal line of business—construction manufacturing and mining equipment—to electronics, software, and logistics. Founded in 1921, Komatsu currently has close to one billion shares outstanding and averages $8 billion in sales annually. The Japanese company's 81 subsidiaries and 27,000 employees carry out the firm's mission throughout the world. Since 1970, Komatsu has established operations in Australia, China, Germany, Hong Kong, Italy, Indonesia, South Africa, and the United States.

From the beginning, Komatsu produced heavy equipment such as sheet-forming presses, farm tractors, bulldozers, forklift trucks, and dump trucks. During the 1960s and 1970s, Komatsu expanded its heavy equipment line to include wheeloaders, excavators, and amphibious bulldozers.

The firm has been recognized throughout the world for its commitment to quality. In 1964, it received the Deming award for quality control, and about two decades later the firm was awarded the world's highest quality control honor, the Japan Quality Control Prize. See the bottom of page 104 and the top of page 105 for selected financial information for Komatsu Ltd., for the period 1977 to 1995.

Caterpillar, Inc.
(000,000s)

Items	1977	1978	1979	1980	1981	1982	1983	1984	1985	1986
Current assets—total	2,628.30	2,606.90	2,932.90	3,544.40	3,433.00	3,383.00	2,915.00	2,982.00	3,363.00	3,813.00
Current liabilities—total	1,237.10	1,386.10	1,711.50	2,369.50	1,197.00	1,576.00	1,939.00	1,742.00	2,180.00	2,392.00
Assets—total	5,031.09	5,403.30	6,098.20	7,284.90	7,201.00	6,968.00	6,223.00	6,016.00	6,288.00	6,866.00
Long-term debt—total	1,018.00	951.90	931.60	960.90	2,389.00	1,894.00	1,384.00	1,177.00	963.00	900.00
Sales (net)	7,219.20	7,613.20	8,597.79	9,154.50	6,469.00	5,424.00	6,576.00	6,725.00	7,321.00	8,180.00
Income before extraordinary items	566.30	491.60	564.80	578.90	(180.00)	(345.00)	(428.00)	198.00	76.00	319.00
Price—close	58.75	54.00	58.00	55.50	40.13	47.25	31.00	42.00	40.13	62.00
Employees	88.01	89.40	81.90	85.92	61.31	58.10	61.62	53.62	53.73	54.46
Research and development expense	163.00	190.50	200.20	226.60	234.00	220.00	231.00	218.00	178.00	159.00
Earnings per share	6.56	5.69	6.53	6.64	(2.04)	(3.74)	(4.47)	2.02	0.77	3.20
Common shares outstanding	86.365	86.434	86.493	87.591	88.266	95.154	96.796	98.379	98.832	101.423

Caterpillar, Inc.
(000,000s)

Items	1987	1988	1989	1990	1991	1992	1993	1994	1995
Current assets—total	5,317.00	5,708.00	5,901.00	5,570.00	5,537.00	6,071.00	7,409.00	7,647.00	8,783.00
Current liabilities—total	3,435.00	3,904.00	4,259.00	3,859.00	4,227.00	4,671.00	5,498.00	6,049.00	7,013.00
Assets—total	9,686.00	10,926.00	11,951.00	12,042.00	13,935.00	14,807.00	16,250.00	16,830.00	18,728.00
Long-term debt—total	1,953.00	2,288.00	2,890.00	3,892.00	4,119.00	3,895.00	4,270.00	3,964.00	4,532.00
Sales (net)	10,435.00	11,126.00	11,436.00	10,182.00	10,194.00	11,615.00	14,328.00	16,072.00	16,522.00
Income before extraordinary items	616.00	497.00	210.00	(404.00)	(218.00)	681.00	955.00	1,136.00	1,361.00
Price—close	63.63	57.88	47.00	43.88	53.63	89.00	55.13	58.75	75.25
Employees	57.95	60.41	58.45	53.64	50.75	51.25	53.99	54.35	57.03
Research and development expense	182.00	235.00	238.00	272.00	310.00	319.00	311.00	375.00	410.00
Earnings per share	6.07	4.90	2.07	(4.00)	(2.16)	6.72	4.70	5.72	7.07
Common shares outstanding	101.414	101.419	100.906	100.912	100.952	101.862	200.442	194.015	190.351

Komatsu, Ltd.—ADR
(000,000s)

Items	1977	1978	1979	1980	1981	1982	1983	1984	1985	1986
Current assets—total	2,460.79	2,156.51	2,720.27	2,663.03	2,677.45	2,489.73	2,472.95	3,405.66	4,279.06	5,997.33
Current liabilities—total	2,321.99	1,975.27	2,433.66	2,373.46	2,170.26	1,968.92	1,859.99	2,573.22	3,112.59	4,303.46
Assets—total	3,809.44	3,303.53	4,072.42	3,988.84	3,943.58	3,828.98	3,745.26	5,017.80	6,225.84	8,491.53
Long-term debt—total	365.31	320.52	307.62	220.20	287.00	247.60	320.33	365.72	412.54	509.72
Sales (net)	2,472.85	2,325.95	3,175.36	3,198.66	3,433.81	3,235.04	2,831.24	3,981.18	4,991.94	6,120.65
Income before extraordinary items	101.12	98.94	136.11	151.17	138.30	113.21	89.85	109.58	93.04	78.55
Price—close	NA	NA	NA	40.00	45.00	46.50	37.88	48.63	61.63	94.25
Employees	22.04	22.09	22.63	23.61	24.65	23.75	23.40	23.23	22.95	22.87
Research and development expense	60.50	52.99	82.73	90.26	131.31	142.19	118.29	136.14	184.22	245.13
Earnings per share	2.84	2.74	3.70	4.00	3.55	2.81	2.16	2.56	2.16	1.84
Common shares outstanding	35.91	36.53	37.11	38.50	39.95	40.46	40.78	41.36	41.57	43.11

Komatsu, Ltd.—ADR
(000,000s)

Items	1987	1988	1989	1990	1991	1992	1993	1994	1995
Current assets—total	6,078.91	5,523.26	6,402.70	6,598.64	6,861.91	8,579.86	11,078.60	9,095.06	7,433.44
Current liabilities—total	3,802.29	3,628.80	3,987.00	4,863.67	4,693.05	6,410.51	8,147.66	6,662.38	5,591.48
Assets—total	8,488.40	7,788.84	9,355.95	10,923.44	11,512.70	13,489.86	17,723.82	14,887.88	12,199.44
Long-term debt—total	959.70	695.57	1,219.14	1,669.84	1,800.24	1,397.82	1,615.52	1,310.36	1,319.27
Sales (net)	5,960.97	5,614.61	7,013.45	6,915.44	7,564.59	8,292.68	10,562.18	9,339.51	8,862.23
Income before extraordinary items	156.64	172.67	221.69	81.94	26.41	24.25	117.53	133.56	146.45
Price—close	139.64	191.50	143.38	116.75	113.12	115.72	NA	NA	NA
Employees	21.63	23.82	24.82	26.06	26.31	28.45	28.04	27.92	27.01
Research and development expense	201.50	192.80	255.31	284.84	281.19	319.55	416.85	336.55	330.26
Earnings per share	3.20	3.36	4.32	1.62	0.52	0.50	2.34	2.66	2.94
Common shares outstanding	45.86	49.53	50.09	50.12	50.13	50.16	50.20	50.20	49.20

Discussion Questions

1. Using the information provided, calculate (if necessary) and graph the following:

    *   Return on assets (ROA)

    *   Return on sales (ROS)

    *   Asset turnover

    *   Firm value (long-term debt + [shares outstanding × end-of-period share price])

    *   Current ratio

    *   Number of employees

    *   Research and development expense

    *   Year-to-year change in earnings per share

2. Using the information in question 1, describe trends and list unusual items. Compare Caterpillar's and Komatsu's financial performance and position.

3. What do the DuPont measures tell you about Caterpillar and Komatsu? DuPont formula: ROA = (net income/sales) / (sales/assets)

4. Explain how the two companies could improve ROA.

Understanding Processes

Case 12.2

Night-Right, Inc.

Modern World Scientist, Issue 10,450; January 1992:

"Scientists at Night-Right, Inc., have discovered a new, all-natural sleeping aid. According to the firm's reports, the compound is extricated from banana skins during the firm's patented manufacturing process. Night-Right's scientists also believe the compound is not habit-forming and has no side effects. The firm's clinical studies show that the new extract, when combined with a carbonated medium such as soda water, provides a refreshing tasty beverage that assists in providing a good night of sleep."

When Marla Frances read this article she couldn't believe her eyes. In fact, she called the magazine *(Modern World Scientist)* to make sure it wasn't a hoax. One of the magazine's editors told her it was true. Marla asked how she could contact the firm. The editor told her it was in Hurricane Lake, Virginia.

Marla immediately called Night-Right and asked whether she could purchase some of the compound. The marketing office told her that Night-Right would soon sell it in carbonated-beverage form. The beverage would be called "Pillo." When she asked to place an order now, she was told that the firm was accepting orders for cases only. Marla ordered two cases and waited eagerly.

Three months later, the cases arrived at Marla's home. She was so excited that she opened one of the cartons, pulled out a can of Pillo, and took a sip. She thought the beverage was so flavorful that it could stand on its own. She felt the new soft drink would succeed even if the sleep feature didn't work. She continued drinking and finished the can within five minutes.

Marla had forgotten all about the drink's natural sedative effect—that is, until she began to feel sleepy, even though it was only 9:00 A.M. When she woke up, she felt great. She was on a high and began to think of ways she could spread the word about the company. Marla entertained notions of owning her own Pillo distributorship.

That afternoon, she called Night-Right. After several minutes of conversation, a company representative told her that the firm had no branches but did have a number of bottling plants around the country. After several more minutes, Marla offered her services to Night-Right. She was hired on the basis of the phone interview and began working at a bottling plant in Little Rock, Arkansas.

Within two years, Marla was plant manager with a salary and a bonus that was tied to the plant's profits. Pillo had two years of steady growth, then sales flattened. The bottling operation remained profitable, but Marla received a below-average bonus which prompted her to investigate how profits were calculated. When she made an inquiry about the firm's financial status, one of the staff accountants sent her the following report.

	Concentrate Producer	**Bottler (Little Rock)**
Sales	100%	100%
Cost of goods sold	21	53
Gross margin	79%	47%
Less:		
Marketing expenses	(40)	(15)
Delivery	(5)	(20)
Administration	(5)	(5)
Net income	19%	7%

Discussion Questions

1. How could Marla improve bottling profits?

2. How could Marla improve bottling profits without changing any operations?

Chapter 13

International Issues

Case 13.1

International Chair Company

International Chair Company, (ICC), is the eighth-largest chair manufacturer in the world. The company assembles the chairs in the United States, but the principal components are manufactured in several different countries.

ICC is known for its high-quality office chair. Last year, the firm's top-of-the-line model was awarded first prize (the Blue Ribbon) at the international office products convention. In addition, ICC's products are consistently ranked number one by J. D. Power and Associates.

In order to ensure its reputation for excellence, ICC has purchased manufacturing companies known for state-of-the-art quality and/or technology with respect to each component. Currently, the foreign companies are wholly-owned subsidiaries of ICC. The subsidiaries are taxed on earnings by the country in which their headquarters and manufacturing facilities are located. In all cases, the administrative and production sites are located in the same country.

When the subsidiaries' after-tax profits are repatriated to the United States in the form of dividends, the dividends are taxed at the U.S. rate. There is no local withholding tax on dividends sent to the United States in any of the foreign jurisdictions.

The manufacturing process consists of five stages. In stages 1 through 4, upholstery is made in Singapore, wheels in Ireland, frames in Germany, and pneumatic controls in

Japan. In the last stage (stage 5), the parts are shipped to the United States where they are assembled in Omaha, Nebraska. ICC pays each subsidiary for the components. The firm manufactures and sells 100,000 chairs annually.

Listed below are tax, cost, and market price data for each of a chair's key parts.

Component	Country	Tax Rate	Cost	Market Price
Upholstery	Singapore	10%	$6.00	$10.00
Wheels	Ireland	5	2.50	5.00
Frame	Germany	45	8.00	14.00
Controls	Japan	40	4.00	8.00
Assembly	United States	30		60.00

The firm's controller, Michelle Fife, is concerned about proposed international transfer pricing legislation. Under the proposed law, firms with activities that fall within the current transfer pricing provisions would be required to select one of the following three transfer prices:

- Market price
- Cost
- Cost plus 20 percent markup

Michelle is not sure how the legislation, if enacted, would affect ICC. With the approval of the firm's CEO, Michelle asked Joanne Fusaro, a Big Five accounting firm tax partner, to help her determine how to deal with the proposed tax rules. Michelle also asked whether she should hire a tax accountant who would handle international tax issues on a daily and permanent basis.

Discussion Questions

1. Calculate the amount of tax owed to each of the five countries and the total tax liability, assuming that all transfer prices are made at:

- Cost
- Cost plus 20 percent markup
- Market price

2. Which price is optimal for the firm?

3. Assume that the firm can choose any of the aforementioned on a selective basis. That is, the firm can choose a different transfer price depending on the tax characteristics of the local jurisdiction. What is the optimal transfer pricing scheme (one that minimizes total tax)?

4. Assume the firm will hire an international tax specialist for a salary that equals half of the difference between the maximum and minimum tax liabilities. How much is the firm willing to pay?

Case 13.2

Financial Measurement: U.S. and Japan

John Jones and Jenny Page met to discuss the impact of accounting differences on traditional financial-oriented measures such as financial ratios. Specifically, they were trying to decide how to convert return on assets (ROA) calculated using Japanese generally accepted accounting principles (GAAP) to ROA using United States GAAP.

John and Jenny were financial analysts for Ventura Capital, Inc., a company that managed investment portfolios for individuals of very high net worth. Since both majored in accounting and minored in finance, the firm gave them assignments that involved financial statement analysis.

John and Jenny both enjoyed quantitative research. With respect to this project, their first move was to consult Ventura's research, which was contained in the firm's online database. After several hours, they came across a Morgan Stanley/Dean Witter report called "Comparing Apple to Apples," that outlined U.S./Japanese GAAP differences. A brief outline of the report follows.

U.S. and Japan Accounting Differences

Item	U.S.	Japan
1. *Consolidation*	Consistency in group accounting policies.	Consistency not required.
	All 50-percent owned subsidiaries must be consolidated.	50-percent owned subsidiaries are not consolidated if profits are immaterial.
2. *Pensions*	Detailed disclosure.	Incomplete disclosure that tends to understate obligation.
3. *Marketable securities*	Some unrealized gains/losses affect income.	Most unrealized gains/losses affect only equity.
4. *Depreciation*	Straight-line is often used.	Many companies use accelerated methods.
5. *Research and development costs*	Expensed.	Some costs are capitalized.

Discussion Questions

1. What should John and Jenny watch out for when they analyze financial statements of Japanese companies?

2. How would the five items in the text above influence the ROA conversion?

3. Is the conversion worth their time?

Chapter 14

Variable Costing

Case 14.1

Aero-Futon, Inc.

Aero-Futon, Inc., (Aero), designs, produces, and sells an inflatable futon bed. It is the only manufacturer of inflatable futons. However, it competes with companies that sell inflatable mattresses. Aero distinguishes itself in the mattress market by producing a product that can be used as a bed, or, after a straightforward adjustment, as an upright couch. Purchasers remark how comfortable both the bed and couch are.

After several years of success, the company is beginning to reach a steady state. More and more, employees are staying with the company, and most of the kinks in the manufacturing system have been worked out. The only thing that causes a major shift in the way the firm does business is demand. Demand for Aero futons not only varies by season, but annual sales have been difficult to predict as well.

Because of these instabilities, Aero's CEO, Dallas Farnsworth, has been reluctant to tie employee bonuses to firm profits. Currently, Dallas and top managers receive a salary, stock options, and a bonus linked to cost control, but Dallas has heard from several managers that the incentive compensation system needs to be altered. Most of the managers are content with the salary and stock awards but do not like the cost-based bonus system. They have told Dallas that the firm must provide incentives to increase profits and should, therefore, tie its bonus system to net income.

Dallas wanted an independent opinion, so he hired Cheryl Nightengale, a Big Five consulting partner specializing in compensation.

When Dallas and Cheryl met for the first time, he informed her of the current situation. In particular, he focused on the managers' growing discontent with the bonus plan. She told him she had dealt with similar situations and found that success or failure of profit-based plans depended on production and sales levels and on the manner in which profits were calculated.

Dallas's background was in marketing; he frequently had to call on accountants to help him analyze the firm's financial statements. It was no surprise, then, that Dallas asked Cheryl to prepare a report explaining in detail what she had just said. Cheryl agreed and asked for cost and production reports for the last two years. The report she received follows:

Cost	1999	2000
Direct materials ($/unit)	$5	$5
Direct labor ($/unit)	$6	$6
Variable overhead ($/unit)	$7	$7
Fixed overhead ($000s)	$200,000	$200,000
Selling and administrative costs ($000s)	$50,000	$50,000
Production ('000s of units)		
Beginning inventory	0	2,000
Units produced	10,000	8,000
Units sold	8,000	10,000
Ending inventory	2,000	0

Cheryl also asked Dallas to give her two feasible sales production forecasts for the next two years. He told her that costs would remain the same and that it was typical for the firm to develop best- and worst-case scenarios:

Best-Case Scenario ('000s of units)

	2001	2002
Beginning inventory	0	0
Units produced	8,000	8,000
Units sold	8,000	8,000
Ending inventory	0	0

Worst-Case Scenario ('000s of units)

	2001	2002
Beginning inventory	0	8,000
Units produced	12,000	4,000
Units sold	4,000	12,000
Ending inventory	8,000	0

Dallas expressed concern that his managers could manipulate the numbers, and he asked Cheryl whether this was possible.

Discussion Questions

1. What is Aero's net income in 1999 and 2000 under absorption costing? Variable costing? Assume the futon sells for $50 per unit.

2. What is Aero's net income in the best- and worst-case scenarios? Under variable and absorption costing?

3. Can Aero's managers manipulate the income numbers? If so, how?

Preparing a Segmented Report

Case 14.2

Tennis Anyone?

Renée and Bill Kustos were child tennis prodigies. The sister and brother twins were born in Noblesville, Kansas, which had a history of producing outstanding tennis players. Renée and Bill were exceptional because they had outstanding physical skills as well as a passion for the sport.

As teenagers, they competed in and won national tennis tournaments. They planned on playing professional tennis, but injuries prevented both of them from becoming international tennis stars. Instead of going on tour, they both opted for college and majored in business.

The twins could no longer play, but their love for the game stayed strong. In order to quench their thirst for the sport, their first jobs after graduating were with competing firms that produced tennis rackets: Bill joined Wilson, and Renée took a job with Prince.

After five years in marketing and another three in management, the Kustos twins left their respective firms and created their own company that designed, manufactured, and sold tennis rackets.

The new firm was called Jolly Kustos, Inc., and the racket lines were JK1, JK2, and JK3. Sales were brisk and grew at a rate of 10 percent each year. Renée and Bill oversaw the company's operations. They hired ex-tennis stars to manage each of the divisions, which were organized by product line with each of the three racket models being the exclusive product of each division.

As time progressed, the twins became increasingly concerned about the performance of the divisions. They called the firm's controller and asked her to send them the previous month's financial results, which are presented here.

	JK1	JK2	JK3
Revenue	$2,500,000	$1,200,000	$600,000
Variable expenses	500,000	250,000	200,000
Controllable fixed expenses	600,000	400,000	175,000
Fixed expense controllable by others	200,000	100,000	50,000

After looking at the information for about an hour, they again called on the controller and asked her to prepare a report that would address the following questions:

- Is the firm profitable?
- Which division is most successful? Least successful?
- Should we eliminate any of the product lines?
- Where should we devote most of our marketing dollars?

Discussion Question

Prepare a report that addresses the aforementioned questions.

Chapter 15

Cost-Volume-Profit Analysis

Case 15.1

Ice Cream Cup

Ice Cream Cup, Inc., is a franchise that specializes in ice cream cones, shakes, and desserts (such as ice cream pies and cakes). Marne Bryers purchased the rights for a store in a town of about 50,000 people. She had plenty of competition, which ranged from yogurt- and custard-based ice cream shops to restaurant franchises such as McDonald's. The local economy was good and growing rapidly due to new firms that provided accounting and billing services to medium- and large-sized telecommunications companies.

Marne was a people person, a natural-born salesperson and manager. In addition, she had very sound business instincts. She worked with a local accountant who kept the business's books and paid the taxes. After several years, though, she felt that she could do the books on her own—particularly because Paul, the accountant, did not provide any assessment regarding business strategy, nor did he help her interpret the reports.

In fact, she began to chart profits and costs on a monthly basis for the three-year period that began when she purchased the business. Her charts revealed some interesting trends. To understand the trends in greater depth, she listed several accounts that varied widely. For example, monthly revenues were as high as $20,000 and as low as $5,000. Several other interesting outcomes are listed here:

Monthly Results

	High	Low
Revenues	$20,000	$5,000
Cost of sales (% of revenues)	40%	20%
Ice cream sold	35 tubs	8 tubs
Salaries	$6,000	$3,800
Utilities and rent	$2,400	$1,800
Net income	$4,000	$(2,000)

She understood that revenues and profits were tied to weather. The high gross revenue month was June, and the low gross month was February. Since the store was located in northern Ohio, it was obvious why the store had more customers and high utility costs in the summer and lower volume and utility expenses in the winter.

What confused Marne was the large fluctuation in cost of sales. She felt that if she could explain why this number varied so greatly, she could improve the store's profit picture. The cost of sales figures were confusing because they did not vary in accordance with the season and weather patterns. Listed below are costs of sales figures (expressed as a percentage of revenues) for the most recent 12-month period.

Month	Cost of Sales (percent of revenues)
January	25%
February	30
March	32
April	40
May	34
June	30
July	28
August	37
September	30
October	27
November	20
December	28

She also listed the products she sold by month. The list is provided below.

| | **Percent of Total Sales** | | |
	Ice Cream Cones	**Sundaes**	**Cakes/Pies**
January	43%	14%	43%
February	48	12	40
March	50	15	35
April	65	15	20
May	52	16	32
June	50	15	35
July	41	18	41
August	60	20	20
September	50	15	35
October	45	15	40
November	40	10	50
December	45	15	40

Discussion Questions

1. Provide a plausible explanation for the variation in cost of sales.

2. Based on the information presented, provide Marne with a feasible strategy.

Case 15.2

Stewart Clothing Company

Stewart Clothing Company manufactures several styles of pants. Demand for Stewart pants is increasing due to the popularity of its golf line. Because of the increase in demand, management is trying to decide how many (if any) of each style of pants to produce.

The company's CEO, Jeff Parr, sincerely believes that the company can meet all demands despite its capacity limitations. Jeff is an optimist; he thinks that if you truly believe, then you can do anything. For example, Jeff has historically shot between 90 and 100 for an 18-hole round. However, one summer, as his story goes, he believed he could average below 90. And, lo and behold, his average that summer was 87!

Jeff called on Leslie Torres, one of the firm's senior accountants, in an effort to resolve the capacity issue. Jeff also called on his senior vice president in charge of marketing, Jim Foley, to help him with the dilemma.

He asked Leslie and Jim to meet him in his office at 9:00 A.M. on the Tuesday following Thanksgiving, which was about a week away. He told them, "Bring all your clubs—you are going to need them! In addition, please bring your most recent budgets and forecasts."

On that Tuesday, Jeff asked Jim for his most recent sales forecast for the upcoming year. The forecast is presented here.

Product	Estimated Demand (units)
Golf Pants–Style 279	50,000
Golf Pants–Style 280	42,000
Golf Pants–Style 281	35,000
Golf Pants–Style 282	40,000
Golf Pants–Style 283	325,000

Jeff then asked Leslie if she knew how much the firm made on the sale of each pair of pants. She told him that 281 had the highest contribution margin and 280 had the lowest. She then handed him a sheet of paper with the following information.

Item	Contribution Margin/Unit
281	$7.56
279	5.20
282	3.00
283	2.80
280	1.90

Jeff remarked, "It's too obvious: let's make lines 281 and 279 and forget about the rest." Jim and Leslie looked at each other and agreed, "We should talk to Shawn first. She has some production data that should be included in our analysis." Jeff nodded and called her on his speakerphone. He asked Shawn to bring him the most recent production budgets.

When Shawn arrived, Jeff told her he needed some important information, then turned to Leslie and Jim and said, "What is the information we need?" Leslie said, "I would like to know how much labor and machine time it takes to make each style." Jim said, "I would like to know how many labor and machine hours are available. What is our production capacity?"

Shawn offered them this table.

Product	Direct Labor Hours per Unit	Machine Hours per Unit
279	0.40	0.10
280	0.25	0.20
281	0.70	0.20
282	0.50	0.10
283	0.20	0.10
Capacity (hours)	130,000	25,000

Jeff turned to the group and said, "Do we have enough information now?" Leslie said, "Almost! I want you to know that all labor is paid $10 per hour."

Discussion Questions

1. Which products should be produced and in what quantity?

2. Using your answer in question 1, how much will the firm make in terms of total contribution margin?

Chapter 16

Relevant Costs

Case 16.1

Short Stories

The Bacon Story

Bacon, Inc., is a food company that sells unique products. Its most popular is a pig for pig roasts. Purchasers of the pig either roast it in the ground (Hawaiian style) or put it on an above-ground rotisserie. Bacon, Inc., ships the slaughtered whole pig in a large crate. Currently, the firm makes its own crates. However, founder and CEO, John Farsical, is considering buying the crates from another company. Bacon's controller has compiled the following data.

	Per Unit	
	Cost to Make	**Cost to Buy**
Direct materials	$ 5	
Direct labor	6	
Variable overhead	2	
Fixed overhead	3	____
	$16	$15

Discussion Question

Should Bacon make or buy?

SIATSO, Inc.
(Should I Accept the Special Order?, Inc.)

SIATSO, Inc., manufactures men's clothing. Its principal markets are in warm climates. The firm has developed a new designer shirt that holds up well in very warm temperatures and normally sells for $25. However, the firm recently received an offer from a national government to buy 10,000 shirts for $20 each. SIATSO's president was presented with the following data relating to the special order.

	Per Unit Cost to Make
Direct materials	$ 8
Direct labor	6
Variable overhead	4
Fixed overhead	2
Allocated corporate overhead	2
Total cost	$22

Discussion Questions

1. Should the firm accept the special order?

2. What is the minimum price the firm should accept?

Droplets, Inc.

Shay Gallagher, owner of Droplets, Inc., faced a very tough decision. She had to decide whether to discontinue her favorite product line, wax candles. Her company had two products, candles and fragrances. The firm's recent financial statements had shown that the perfume segment was profitable while the candle division was generating a loss. The financial statement is presented here.

	Perfume	Candles
Sales	$200,000	$300,000
Cost of goods sold	(150,000)	(250,000)
Gross margin	$ 50,000	$ 50,000
Allocated corporate overhead	(40,000)	(60,000)
Net income	$ 10,000	$ (10,000)

Discussion Question

Should the candle division be dropped?

Campus Orchards

Campus Orchards (Campus) grows and sells apples. The firm also produces and sells applesauce. The company has been in business for several years and is trying to decide whether it should update its applesauce manufacturing facility. Johnny Lane, the firm's controller, believes that Campus should sell apples and not applesauce. His wife, Molly, the president of Campus, strongly disagrees. She said, "What? Sell apples and not applesauce? I don't want to break with tradition." After a Sunday dinner, the couple looked over the following data in an effort to resolve their disagreement.

	Sales Price	Additional Manufacturing Costs
Apples	$2.00	$1.00
Applesauce	$3.50	$2.00

Discussion Question

Should Campus sell apples or applesauce?

The Shirts of Company C

Company C produces and sells T-shirts, sweatshirts, and jackets. The firm's product is sold by university bookstores throughout the country. Company C's products have become so popular that, this year, demand exceeded capacity for the first time since the company was formed. The firm's founder, Ellie Tooksbury, is trying to decide which product line should be produced with the available machine capacity. Her assistant, Sharon Bomin, has provided her with the following information.

	T-shirts	Sweatshirts	Jackets
Sales price per unit	$20	$30	$40
Variable costs per unit	(15)	(20)	(20)
Fixed costs per unit	—	(5)	(15)
Profit per unit	$ 5	$ 5	$ 5
Machine hours per unit	5	5	5
Demand	1,000	5,000	10,000
Total machine time available	10,000 hours		

Discussion Questions

1. Which product line(s) should be produced? How much will the firm make in terms of contribution margin?

2. How much machine time would be needed to produce enough to meet demand for three products?

Case 16.2

Private Club Eatery

Private Club Eatery, (PCE), was, in part, a misnomer. It was a restaurant, but it also had a large bar. It was not private; it was open to the public. In addition, it was not a club that had members; its members were current diners and imbibers.

PCE was established in 1998 by husband and wife owners Carl and Carla Piteli. They wanted to build a restaurant and bar that would be the cornerstone of shopping malls in affluent areas. They thought PCE would appeal to several segments of the population: weekly and weekend shoppers who wanted high-quality lunch experiences; businesspeople who conducted business via lunches; local residents who wanted a fine-dining experience; and young adults who enjoyed winding down after work.

The couple's first and only restaurant was built in a mall in Oak Town, Illinois. The restaurant had two floors. The first level had a long bar that occupied two-thirds of the floor space. The remaining one-third of the first floor had tables for lunch and dinner. The second floor had no bar facilities, just tables for eating.

As building progressed, the couple began thinking about their hiring strategy. They believed they would have to compete for the same food and beverage employees who worked at other high-end restaurants. They felt strongly that the restaurant's success would depend largely on the quality of service provided by its servers, and, therefore, were willing to pay premium wages.

Carl and Carla researched the issue and discovered that similar restaurants paid a wage of $5-6 per hour, plus tips. The couple also gathered the following data and made the forecasts provided here.

	Competition			Private Club
	High	**Low**	**Average**	**Private Club**
Hourly wage	$6	$5	$5.50	$?
Number of patrons served lunch (6 hours)	200	100	160	140
Number of patrons served dinner (6 hours)	180	60	80	120
Average bill per patron—lunch (excludes alcohol)	$25	$14	$21	$20
Average bill per patron—dinner (excludes alcohol)	$30	$17	$22	$25
Bar patrons—lunch				
At bar	20	0	8	45
At tables	25	0	12	25
Bar patrons—dinner				
At bar	30	0	15	70
At tables	35	0	25	50
Average bar tab per patron—lunch				
At bar	$8	$0	$6	$5
At tables	$8	$0	$4	$5
Average bar tab per patron—dinner				
At bar	$10	$0	$8	$8
At tables	$12	$0	$4	$8

After Carl and Carla looked at the information, they began questioning whether it would be in their best interest to outbid other restaurants by increasing the hourly wage and/or by guaranteeing a minimum tip of 15 percent on food and beverage charges.

Discussion Questions

1. If the Pitelis' strategy is to compete for the highest-paid workers, provide potential compensation packages.

2. If the Pitelis' strategy is to provide their employees with average compensation, provide potential compensation packages.

3. What strategy would you suggest?

Chapter 17

Capital Budgeting

Case 17.1

The Coffee Truck

Bryson Jumers, CEO of CleanUp, Inc., (CleanUp), was contemplating a change. He thought that if he could improve worker morale, his labor force would be more efficient. Bryson and his wife, Lois, thought employees would like free coffee before and during work hours. However, delivering hot coffee to workers would be difficult as job sites changed on a regular basis.

CleanUp provided cleaning services ranging from waste hauling to leaf blowing. The company had a major contract with the local university's athletic department. CleanUp was especially good at cleaning athletic facilities after major sporting events. Immediately following an event, CleanUp employees would begin removing everything from candy wrappers to popcorn containers from the premises. This was a particularly difficult task because such items tended to get caught between chairs or stuck on the ground after becoming pressed into the concrete. The workers most dreaded "peanut brittle," which was what they labeled the combination of peanuts and soft drinks. It was very difficult to remove from floors.

Bryson thought if he could purchase a truck outfitted to produce coffee on a 24–hour basis, he could serve employees on all active sites. Lisa and Bryson performed some quick calculations that led them to believe that all sites could be served if stops at each site were limited to 15 minutes.

Bryson was about to go to a local bank for a loan that would allow him to expand operations to another university community. He was worried about how the coffee truck purchase would affect the firm's financial statements. However, he was hopeful that cash saved via tax deductions would sufficiently improve the firm's operating cash flows.

Bryson called upon his accountant, Mack Donald, to help him prepare pro-forma financial statements under the "go" and "no go" assumptions. In this case, "go" meant CleanUp would purchase the truck.

Mack asked Bryson to send him the information relating to the purchase, which is shown here.

Coffee Truck

Asset cost	$21,000
Salvage (estimated)	$1,000
Useful life	5 years

Discussion Questions

1. Calculate annual depreciation using straight-line, double-declining balance, and sum-of-the-years digits methods. Which method is best for Bryson?

2. Calculate annual depreciation for tax purposes assuming the tax amount is calculated using double-declining balance assuming no salvage and half-year convention.

3. Should Bryson make the purchase? Should net present value analysis be used in this instance?

Comparing Payback, Accounting Rate of Return, and NPV Analysis

---

Case 17.2

Income By Any Other Method

Judy thought she was about to stump JoAnne. This was a brain teaser (maybe). Using the following information, Judy asked JoAnne to calculate annual and total economic income, accrual income, and cash income.

Initial investment	$69,302.11 (made in 1999)
Depreciation method	Straight-line
Useful life	4 years
Salvage	0
Discount rate	6%

Year	Cash Flow
1999	$20,000
2000	20,000
2001	20,000
2002	20,000

Judy said to JoAnne, "Before you get started, I should tell you that income by any other method will always come out the same." Judy told JoAnne to calculate the payback period, accounting rate of return, and net present value assuming the machine costs $80,000.

Discussion Questions

1. Calculate annual and total economic, accrual, and cash income.

2. Calculate the payback period, accounting rate of return, and net present value assuming the equipment costs $69,302.11.

3. Calculate the payback period, accounting rate of return, and net present value assuming the equipment costs $80,000.

Case 17.3

The Congressman

Paul Gray was recently elected to the United States House of Representatives. Paul's first action was to hire a chief of staff to manage his office and affairs on a daily basis. Paul turned to his high school sweetheart, Rebecca Turner, for help. He asked whether she would fill the position for the next two years. Rebecca told him she would request a leave of absence from her employer, Arthur Andersen. Rebecca was a tax partner in the Washington, D.C., office.

Within a couple of weeks, Rebecca received approval from headquarters. She quickly called Paul and accepted the job offer.

Paul had almost no understanding of tax, but he felt he must learn quickly since a call for a vote concerning tax legislation was expected to occur within the next six weeks. In particular, Paul was concerned about the proposed changes in the accelerated depreciation provisions.

He called Rebecca into his office and asked her what the following statement meant: Accelerated tax depreciation is double-declining balance, with no salvage, half-year convention, with a switch to straight-line.

Rebecca told him the only way to really understand tax depreciation is to derive the tax tables.

Discussion Questions

1. Using the information from the case, derive the tax tables for three- and five-year property.

2. Why did Congress adopt any form of accelerated depreciation? The half-year convention? A depreciation law that did not consider salvage value?

Chapter 18

Inventory

Case 18.1

He Said, She Said

He said it didn't matter; she said it did. It was a classic battle between two accountants over debits and credits. He was on the left. She was on the right. We are not talking politics here (or are we?). What is at issue relates to one of the most important accounting rules in the history of humanity. A rule that relates to cost of goods sold. A rule that governs how to value inventory. A rule that is on the tip of every businessperson's tongue. Yes, we are talking about LIFO and FIFO.

Roy thought that—given the new purchasing, sales, and production strategy—inventory method choice (that is, LIFO, FIFO, or weighted average) would not change net income. Ellen disagreed and asked for the records that are presented here. There was no beginning inventory.

Date	Layer	Units Purchased	Price	Cost	Units Sold
1/1	#1	5,000	$4.00	$20,000	
1/9					3,000
1/10	#2	6,000	$5.00	$30,000	
1/12					2,000
1/20					4,000
1/30	#3	1,000	$10.00	$10,000	

Ellen said, "Look, Roy, I don't want to be mean, but I think you are being obtuse." She continued, "Although we sold all goods for $10, we purchased them for different amounts."

Roy nodded and said, "I agree, but next month we are moving to a just-in-time inventory production method. Now do you agree with me?"

Discussion Questions

1. Calculate net income on ending inventory for January using LIFO, FIFO, and weighted average cost flow assumptions. The company uses a periodic inventory system.

2. Now assume purchases equal sales. Calculate net income using all three cost flow assumptions.

3. Who is correct: Ellen or Roy?

Case 18.2

Ashtray City, Inc.

Char and Nick were college sweethearts in business making psychedelic ashtrays. It was their own home-grown business. When the couple received an order, Char prepared their apartment for the manufacturing process. On average, this took eight minutes. Then, Nick formed clay in various shapes (whatever suited him at the time). The shaping process lasted four minutes.

When he was finished, Char turned on the kiln and placed the clay form(s) in it. This process lasted about two minutes. The ashtrays baked for ten minutes and cooled for four. Nick then placed them in boxes and set them on the floor. This took about two minutes.

During the previous holiday season, the couple had not been able to produce enough to meet demand. This was because, in part, their kiln could fire only one ashtray at a time. The couple made $10 per tray (contribution margin).

Nick and Char had to consider investing in a new kiln that would cost about $1,400. It, too, would hold only one ashtray at a time. They also considered buying another type of kiln that held two ashtrays at a time. Its price was $1,800.

They felt they could work 20 hours a week for three weeks during December.

Discussion Questions

1. Should they invest in a new kiln? If so, which one?